Petar Ian

WHERE TO WATCH
BIRDS
IN BULGARIA

BSPB Popular Series No. 1

Illustrations by
Georgi Pchelarov

1996

PENSOFT

AN INTERNATIONAL PUBLISHING HOUSE IN ALL FIELDS OF LIFE & ENVIRONMENTAL SCIENCES

Acad. G. Bonchev Str., Bl. 6
1113 Sofia, Bulgaria
Tel./Fax +359-2-7133460
E-mail: pensoft@main.infotel.bg

Editors: *Dr. S. Golovatch & Dr. L. Penev*
Graphic design: *T. Bachvarova & Dr. D. Dobrev*
Cover design: *Dr. D. Dobrev*

Printed by the Printing-office of "Prof. Marin Drinov" Academic
Publishing House
Sofia, December 1996

Foreword

It is beyond doubt that birds have the most numerous crowds of admirers all over the world. Indeed, one can talk about birds only using big words. They are "super" as the young people's jargon has it nowadays. But what about identifying difficult species and groups? One should certainly have a very well-trained eye and a lot of knowledge about birds. And to tell apart different species only by listening to their songs you'll have to have a very keen hearing. This is the reason why birds are not only an attraction but a challenge as well. This is the reason, too why the bird lovers throughout the world are so interesting and engaging persons.

During all seasons birdwatchers, obsessed of their love, shoulder up telescopes and binoculars and dedicated to their favorites every free minute. And what about holidays! They are carefully planned, long before the time comes, in full detail. Birdwatchers select for their holidays the most interesting and rewarding bird areas. In this respect Bulgaria indeed has something to offer. Its central location on the Balkan Peninsula, its highly diverse lay and vegetation, the Mediterranean influence in the southern regions of the country, the unique flora of Strandzha mountain, the alpine belt in the high mountains, etc., etc. have created a real diversity of birdlife. So far the presence of 367 species of birds have been recorded for Bulgaria 59 of which have been observed for the first time only during the last 50 years. Two of the main migratory flyways for migrating birds from Eastern Europe-the Via Pontica and the Via Aristotelis cross the country. The huge flocks of migrating White Storks at Burgas is an impressive sight one remembers for life. And the migration over Cape Emine? If you are lucky enough and have good weather during your stay at the Cape you can look straight at the eyes the flying over your head Black Storks, Pelicans and raptors. One can hardly ever forget the sight of scores of hundreds exhausted Bee Eaters perching on all shrubs for a short respite. Their brightly colored feathers shine like so many gems in spite of the poor light and the drizzle - hundreds of gems in your telescope! Only the birdwatchers can feel the excitement of such an experience. The winter here about is not a dead season when the only comfort for the bird lovers is to watch again and again the slides taken in the spring and summer. Quite to the contrary! Bulgaria offers wintering grounds for many a species and our wetlands in particular are full of birds. No advertisement is necessary but I simply cannot desist from only mentioning the area of Shabla and Durankulak lakes where winters almost the whole population of the globally threatened Red-breasted Goose. The noise and flurry of thousands of Geese taking off from the lakes with the rising sun in the background and the nipping cold ... no, this is not a thing to narrate, one should experience it on the spot. There are hundreds such places in Bulgaria. So far a good and intelligently written guide was missing. Now you have it in your hands. It was written by an excellent ornithologists, expert on the Bulgarian avifauna and the Important Bird Areas in this country. I believe that this book will become an inseparable companion to anybody who wish to feel the nature and wildlife of Bulgaria and spend unforgettable hours with its birds. This book, I hope, will also help preserve this wealth because it belongs not only to us but to the whole world. When we happen to visit the places described in the book let not forget that we are not only friends of the birds but good husbands as well and let behave as such, always caring for the future, ours and of the wildlife of the planet. Only in this way can we contribute to the preservation and protection of our common nature heritage and the birds in particular.

Despite the efforts exerted by Bulgarian conservationists, the negative processes typical for the whole of Europe do not pass over Bulgaria, too. While the populations of many species of birds are still stable, many others have shown negative trends or have actually decreased. So we too, have our problems and concerns but we do our best to preserve the fascination of our country and the birds that live in it for all their present and future admirers that this book will certainly create.

Bozhidar Ivanov, BSPB President

Contents

Acknowledgements

Besides the fact that there are several books describing birding sites in Bulgaria, the present guide is completely new and it accumulates an incredible amount of original information. Of course, such a serious work could not have been done by a single person. That is why I would like to try to express my thanks to the people without which this great task would not have been possible. Without any doubt, some of them will be missed and I would like to thank all of you who will not find their names here, but certainly will have contribution to it. Sincere gratitude to hundreds of birdwatchers from many countries, who provided me during the last 12 years with the great chance and pleasure to become familiar to and learn the secrets of birdwatching tourism. Many thanks to all of them also for the opportunities which this activity new to my country gives for sustainable development of tourism in Bulgaria and, particularly, for the preservation of its rich biological diversity during the coming years of development. It is difficult to mention all names of excellent and keen birders and other people, but without any doubts among them are the names of Ann and Bob Scott (RSPB), who started the development of this activity in Bulgaria after their first visit in 1982, of Maurice Waterhouse (RSPB), who re-charged many of us with his optimism and conservation knowledge during his visits every year, as well as of Laurence Rose (RSPB), James Cadbury (RSPB), Carl Nicholson (RSPB), Tony O'Neel (RSPB), Carol Winder (RSPB), Prof. Hans Jornvall (Karolinska Institute, Stockholm), Brian Little (BTO), Graham Elliott (RSPB), Edgar Kesteloot (Reserves Naturelles et Ornithologiques de Belgique), Robert Axworty (RSPB), Jan Bos (Stichting Natuurreizen), Major Timoty Hallchurch MBE (Army Ornithological Society) and many others. I'm extremely thankful to all my colleague ornithologists who have shared with me important informations and knowledge on the location of interesting birds and/or helping me in other ways during the trips: Lyubo Profirov, the Bulgarian pioneer in ornithological guiding, Dimitar Georgiev, Bozhidar Ivanov, Tzeno Petrov, Kamen Ruskov, etc. Probably here is the place to thank also the tourist guides and experts, with whom it was so pleasant to work. I shall never forget Svidna Nashkova, Julia Stoianova, Daniela Kotzeva, Emilia Neykova, Svetla Peicheva, Monika Filkova, Rumen Khristov, Radostina Konstantinova, as well as all kind people at the places which our groups passed through during the trips.

Gratitude to all colleagues, who have contributed in different ways to a better quality of this book, and, especially, to Vlado Pomakov, Pavlin Todorov, Bozhidar Ivanov, Lyubo Profirov, Dimitar Georgiev, Kamen Ruskov, Tzeno Petrov, Milen Marinov, Boris Barov, as well as to all other people, without whose efforts and professionalism the book would have looked very different.

Special thanks to the Royal Society for the Protection of Birds, which provided us during all these years with the last nature conservation know-how and which actually has been an example and an initiator of the first effective field nature conservation activities in Bulgaria. Most of this would have been impossible without the initiative of Ita Purton, Secretary of the British-Bulgarian Friendship Society, who found the courage to start organising birdwatching tourism during the years when the Iron Curtain made this almost impossible.

Sincere thanks to the Bulgarian Society for the Protection of Birds for the contribution to this book and for its strong efforts to contribute to the right and sustainable development of eco-tourism to the benefit of people and.nature.

Many thanks to all professionals, for their work on the not easy a task of editing the book, and, especially so, to Dr. Lyubomir Penev, the Chief Editor of Pensoft *Publishers*, to Dr. Sergei Golovatch (Moscow), Tony Bachavarova and Dr. Dobrin Dobrev who are responsible for the excellent quality of this book.

It is my duty to express deep gratitude to my friend Georgi Pchelarov, the top Bulgarian artist animalist, for the brilliant pictures, without which the book would have been too simple.

No words can express my thankfulness to my wife Lyudmila and to our son Kiril, without the understanding, daily support and help of which during the trips and the work on the book it would have been impossible to write it.

Introduction

In 1969, when I started my every day's bird records near the small town of Krumovgrad, the Egyptian Vulture was the first bird which „entered" my notebook. It was normal for me all people in the town to consider my activity unique for Krumovgrad at that time as something strange, or, in the best case, as a temporary interest of a 15-year old boy. During all other following years my fellow citizens slowly changed their opinions about the activity strange and nameless for them of birdwatching, and the first signs of some recognition were visible only after I had completed my PhD in 1983, when I started to work in a respectable scientific research institute and, especially, after my regular appearances on the National TV, Radio and press. But even then there were my fellow townsmen who asked me to make something to encourage an industrial development of the Krumovgrad area. I think that even now most of these very nice and kind people do not understand that they actually live in a real Eldorado and they walk upon gold every day, even without noticing it.

What does this gold look like? The Eastern Rhodopi, in the central part of which Krumovgrad is situated, is one of the richest places in Europe from a point of view of biodiversity. I shall not mention how many interesting or endemic plants, invertebrates, fishes, amphibians, reptiles and mammals occur there. This can be seen on the map of the Bulgarian National Strategy for Biodiversity Conservation as one of the most deeply coloured areas of the country. During the last decades, more than 270 species of birds have been recorded in this mountain. There are 11 Globally Endangered Species among them, but even more interesting is that birds typical for North Europe, such as the Black-throated Diver *Gavia arctica,* can be seen at the same time with birds, which range is Mediterranean, such as the Black Vulture *Aegypius monachus.* The same can be said for some wetland birds, such as the Night Heron *Nycticorax nycticorax,* living in the vicinity of rocky birds, such as the Long-legged Buzzard *Buteo rufinus,* woodland birds such as the Masked Shrike *Lanius nubicus,* and dry bushland birds, such as the Sardinian Warbler *Sylvia melanocephala.* Many others are merits of this paradise mountain, but none of them can be ignored. There are very few areas in Europe, where 34 of all 38 species of Birds of Prey can be seen together, in good numbers, like in the Eastern Rhodopi. And last but not least, this is an area where you can feel the real spirit of wild nature. Time seems to have stopped centuries ago and, in large areas, you can forget about the existence not only of many attributes of civilisation, such as artificial noises, rush, industrial smoke, but you can forget even about the existence of civilisation itself...

All this and many other things, such as the completely clean products of the area for example, are something normal and in the nature of things for local people. It is difficult for many of them to accept, that these things are not the same everywhere. Nobody has ever explained them that this richness can serve not only to themselves, but it can be „sold" in a soft way (but with no less profit) to other people, who already do not have it and who are happy to buy these lost values of an advanced civilisation. That not only they themselves, but also their grandchildren can have solid and sustainable profit from a properly developed touristic industry, based on well-preserved natural richness.

After numerous attempts to find the most effective ways to the long-term nature conservation, we have arrived to the conclusion that it is impossible without a properly situated and sustainable eco-tourism as a motivation for large groups of local people to preserve their natural values, which cannot be covered by protected areas and by a real enforcement of the Law.

I was surprised to find how quickly local people understood and accepted my birdwatching, especially when I did this together with groups of fellows from the BSPB or with foreign tourists. Our last conversations with local people and representatives of local administrations showed that the idea for sustainable „green", or „eco"-tourism was well known and highly appreciated by them. Little by little they started noticing the gold under their feet. And this can be seen everywhere in the country. Put in the right way, it can be the greatest chance for the excellent Bulgarian nature. This makes me remain with clean conscience when thinking about possible accusations. I really believe that this book can be a modest contribution to a better future of people and birds and nature!

Sofia, 21.12.1995

Bulgarian Society for the Protection of Birds
BirdLife Bulgaria

The Bulgarian Society for the Protection of Birds (BSPB) (Registered Charity 122/26.12.1988) was founded in 1988 as a virtually orientated grass-root nature conservation organization, the first one of this kind in Bulgaria after the totalitarianism period. Its main aim is preservation of the birds, their habitats and biodiversity as a whole. BSBP is one of the few membership based nature conservation societies in Bulgaria, which have 16 regional branches in all major towns and regions of the country. There are several main principles which the BSPB has established in its work:
– democratic principles as a base for running the Society
– positivistic attitude to the process of resolving the increasing conservation problems in Bulgaria and cooperation with both governmental and non-governmental nature conservation organizations;
– broader vision for Nature conservation (besides the name of the Society, it is in fact a Nature conservation organization);
– strong scientific capacity and approaches of the Society (besides the top Bulgarian ornithologists, many other respectable scientists from other fields of knowledge take part in BSPB work);
– orientation to particularly practical and visible results for Nature from the Society's work;
– gaining public support for the conservation ideas and actions through making local people involved in the conservation activities and motivating them for the preservation of biodiversity;
– protecting the BSPB from the negative features of the rules and principles of the totalitarianism period, from the negative tendencies of the transition period and building it up as a transparent and clean organization;
– avoiding any political partiality and keeping the Society politically independent.

These principles, the strong internal motivation of the Society members and activists, the most modern approaches to nature conservation (developed in an appropriate strategy and action programme), have allowed the BSPB to gain results unachievable until now for the country. For first time a species extinct from Bulgaria, the Black Vulture *Aegypius monachus*, has been restored as a breeding species after decades of absence. The Bulgarian population of the Griffon Vulture *Gyps fulvus* has increased from 1-4 to 12-16 fledglings per year, the breeding colony of the Dalmatian Pelican *Pelecanus crispus* was saved in the most critical period of the Srebarna Biosphere Reserve. Large-scale management activities have been successfully completed in several internationally important reserves and other territories of high biodiversity interest, and this was in fact the start of a real nature conservation management activity in Bulgaria. This has created public interest and participation in the Society's activities unusually high for Bulgaria. These serious and really practical results for Bulgarian Nature and the overall image of the BSPB have contributed to an extremely high prestige and recognition of this organization within the country and abroad. The BSPB was officially invited by the Ministry of Environment to take part in the elaboration of a National Strategy for Biodiversity Conservation (1993), later on in the development and implementation of a National Action Plan for the Conservation of the Most Important Wetlands in Bulgaria (1994), in the GEF Project for the Conservation of Biodiversity (1994), etc. Many of the activities of the BSPB are examples of good cooperation between the Society and the Ministry of Environment, the Ministry (Committee) of Forests with virtually all really active nature conservation NGOs in Bulgaria. Actually the BSPB carries out the main practical nature conservation activities in Bulgaria: real management of some of the most important nature reserves and high biodiversity areas (including the establishment of artificial islands and other constructions), the national action plans for the Globally Threatened Species of birds, including a programme for artificial upfeeding of scavenging birds, the national monitoring of bird populations (including a mid-winter count of Waterfowl), etc.

The BSPB has become recognized also by the oldest international conservation organization – BirdLife International – which has chosen the BSPB as its Partner for Bulgaria and, thanks to this, ensured the extremely high standard of the Society's work. There are other examples of international recognition of the BSPB, such as its high confidence of the Swiss Government, which assigned to the Society two of its 8 Biodiversity Conservation Projects in Bulgaria (the other 6 were entrusted to the Ministry of the Environment), the BSPB was the winner of the National Award for 1996 of Henry Ford European Conservation Awards, as well as the only Bulgarian NGO invited by the PHARE Programme to participate in the elaboration of the Biomonitoring Programme for Bulgaria.

The Bulgarian Society for the Protection of Birds pursues a programme of:

– **field conservation actions** to improve the living conditions for species, sites and habitats and for biodiversity as a whole;

– **scientific research and analysis** to identify and monitor the

status of, trends and conservation needs in different representatives of biodiversity;
    – **network and capacity building** to expand and strengthen the conservation activities and to increase the results for nature;
    – **advocacy and policy development** to promote the conservation of birds and of biodiversity in general through sustainability in the use of all natural resources.

    The BSPB is deeply involved in the development of eco-tourism in Bulgaria. Virtually no birdwatching groups until now have been on a trip in Bulgaria without birder guides from the Society. A list of about 220 species for only two weeks, is something usual for the groups guided by experts from our Society. An active attitude to the right development of this very important activity is connected in the direct presence in this field through the BSPB company Neophron Ltd. (part of the activities of which are of touristic character), as well as through the intensive work of the BSPB with various organizations, companies and tour operators. Our philosophy is based on the strong belief that one of the most effective ways to preserve the natural values is to provide opportunities to local people to have direct income from their sustainable, „soft" touristic use. Having direct interest from tourists coming to see the Black Stork *Ciconia nigra*'s nest, even the local children will be the best guards of it, and they will need very few additional knowledge and resources to ensure its existence in a long-term perspective. This is our message to all of you, have in mind this, and your contribution to the preservation of Bulgaria's nature will be guaranteed.
    The Bulgarian Society for the Protection of Birds/BirdLife Bulgaria is working hard to build up its financial self-sustainability, and eco-tourism is one of the perspectives in this respect. To preserve the still extremely rich biodiversity of Bulgaria during the coming years of strong development of the country, we should be very strong financially. An effective nature conservation activity (which except for all other is prerequisite to a successful eco-tourism) is not a cheap thing. Any contribution to this will be highly appreciated. If Bulgaria remains in the focus of your birding interests, if you need current information on its wonderful wildlife and on conservation activities, the best way is to become a BSPB member. Besides the opportunity for direct contact, you will receive all this information with an English version of the BSPB Newsletter „*Neophron*", which is sent to every overseas member.

    Welcome to birding, welcome to the preservation of Bulgaria's biodiversity!

A little about Bulgaria

Deciding to visit Bulgaria you will certainly get somewhat informed in advance about the country. There are several new tourist guides of Bulgaria, available in most European book stores and according to which this very old land is not only a territory where people stalk with a dangerous umbrella in the hand or plot against Pope's life, but also smile, take pleasure in helping you in need, working for a better future of themselves and their country... You will be surprised to find there mysteries of an actually unknown country, mysteries of its archaeology and history, of its traditions, national culture, kitchen and, of course, you will be shocked to discover so wild nature areas, unbelievable for Europe for the end of the 20th Century! So we shall not try to repeat these guides. Instead we would like to give you the most basic information which will serve you for a better and easier organisation of your visit to Bulgaria.

Geography: Bulgaria is situated in southeastern Europe, covering 110 993 square km of the eastern side of the Balkan Peninsula. The Danube forms a natural frontier with Rumania to the north, Bulgaria borders Greece and Turkey to the south, Serbia and Macedonia to the west, and Black Sea to the east. The landscape is extremely varied: vast plains alternate with rolling hills, deep river valleys, mountain ranges and massifs, most prominent among which are the Balkan Range (Stara Planina), the Rhodopi, Rila and Pirin mountains. There are altitudes from sea level up to 2 925 m a.s.l. (peak Musala in Rila Mountain, which is the highest in the Balkan Peninsula), the average altitude is 470 m. From a birdwatcher's point of view, use the unique opportunity to be near the Polar Circle (to see the Three-toed Woodpecker in the forests over the Rila Monastery) and, within less than an hour driving, to be in the Mediterranean (to see the Blue Rock Thrush at Kresna Gorge, some 50 km from the same place). You can be at a sea beach with all typical birds here, and only a few hours later to be at 3 000 m a.s.l. with all typical birds there, passing meantime through habitats typical at least for three biogeographical zones. It is useful to know that, due to the excellent geographical position of Bulgaria at the crossroads between Europe and Asia Minor and between the South Russian steppes and the Mediterranean, there are extremely high numbers of birds usually known as rarities" all in most of the other European countries. As you will see from the list of Bulgarian birds at the end of this book, there have been recorded almost 400 bird species. For many of them, Bulgaria is the closest and easiest country they to be seen by West Europeans. Only a few of them seem enough to make twitching every twitcher, having self-respect: the Red-breasted Goose (*Branta ruficollis*), the Isabelline Wheatear (*Oenanthe isabellina*), the Paddyfield Warbler (*Acrocephalus agricola*), the Semi-collared Flycatcher (*Ficedula semitorguata*), the Masked Shrike (*Lanius nubicus*), etc.

Climate: The climate is moderate continental, with Mediterranean influence in the southern regions (2 000 to 2 400 hours of sunlight per year), and a pronounced mountain climate at altitudes of 900 m a.s.l. and above. The Black Sea brings a mild climate to the eastern parts of the country. Here the winter temperatures may be as high as 15°C, while the summer temperatures rarely exceed 25°-26°C. There are distinctive spring, summer, autumn and winter. Take in consideration that, when in the beginning of June at the Black Sea coast, it is just the time for swimming, in the high mountains it can be snowing and you will need gloves to keep the binoculars!

Population: Bulgaria has a population of 8 519 155 people. The mean population density is 80 per square km. The average age in years is 37,5. There are large areas with almost no people and, as a rule, nature is very well-preserved there. But many interesting birds can be seen even in the places with the highest population density. According to one our study, the city of Sofia is a site of this size (181 square km) the most rich in birds in Bulgaria, with 260 bird species, 131 of which are breeding! So, do not underestimate the settlements. In some of Sofia's parks you can find even such birds as the Levant Sparrowhawk (*Accipiter brevipes*) or the Black Woodpecker (*Dryocopus martius*), and in the meadows only a few kilometres away from the centre, you can have the pleasure to listen to the fascinating voice of some of more than 15 Corncrakes (*Crex crex*), calling without worry that they belong to a Globally Threatened Species!

Main dates in the history: For historians, history has nothing to do with birds. Nevertheless, images of such birds as vultures, eagles and some others can be found at many historical places, on coins, icons. The basic dates of Bulgarian history can be simply presented as follows:

>   IV Millennium BC: The oldest golden items found at a necropolis near Varna;
>   II Millennium BC - year 46 BC: A very high-level Tracian culture, with traces in many tombs, mounds and treasures;
>   681 Khan Asparukh founds the Bulgarian State;

863 The brothers Cyril and Methodi create the Slavonic (Cyrillic) alphabet, spread later on by their students to other East European countries;

865 Tsar Boris introduces Christianity as an official religion in Bulgaria;

1259 Economic and cultural upsurge, the first Renaissance icons of the Boyana Church;

1396 The Bulgarian Kingdom falls to the invading Ottoman Turks whose rule lasts for five centuries;

1876 The April Uprising, the biggest popular rebellion against the Ottoman rule, is brutally suppressed. The „Bulgarian atrocities" awaken horror throughout Europe;

1878 Bulgaria regains its freedom following the successful outcome of the Russian-Turkish War;

1878-1944 Third Bulgarian Kingdom, a normal economy and political development of the country;

1944-1989 The country is under the „Soviet" rules of political and economic life;

since 1989 On a way to the integration with other European countries.

Capital: Sofia (population about 1 200 000 people).

Principal Black Sea ports: Varna and Burgas

Checkpoints at the borders:

with Serbia:	Kalotina
	Vrashka Chuka
	Bregovo
with Macedonia:	Gyueshevo
	Zlatarevo
with Greece:	Kulata
	Svilengrad
with Turkey:	Kapitan Andreevo
	Malko Tarnovo
with Rumania:	Vidin
	Oryakhovo
	Ruse
	Silistra
	Kardam
	Durankulak

International Airports: Sofia, Varna, Burgas

Time: Time difference with GMT is 2 hours. Like in most European countries, local „Summer Time" is introduced from the beginning of April to the end of September (GMT + 3 hours).

Currency: lev (equal to 100 stotinki)

Official holidays:
1 January — New Year's Day
3 March — Liberation from the Ottoman rule
second weekend of April — Easter
1 May — International Day of Labour
24 May — Day of the Slav Script
25, 26 December — Christmas

Roads: movement on the right; restrictions in towns — 50 km/h, outside towns — 90 km/h, on highways — 120 km/h

Electricity: 220 V, 50 Hz

Credit Cards: American Express, Eurocard, Mastercard, Visa

Health care: There exist international agreements on free-of-charge health care for most countries. Please check.

Telephone links: There are automatic telephone connections with the whole world. Important phone numbers are:

Ambulance	**150**
Fire	**160**
Police	**166**
Road help	**146**
Taxi	**142**
Sofia Railway Station	**3 11 11**
Sofia Airport domestic	**72 24 14**
international	**72 06 72**
International calls	**0123**

Peculiar feature: Do not get confused by the meaning of the Bulgarian nod which may be the exact opposite of what you expect. By virtue of a long-established national ideosyncrasy, many Bulgarians shake their heads when they mean „yes", and nod when they mean „no". As a matter of fact, you will find that many others indicate agreement or disagreement in a way you would consider quite normal.

How to make your birding in Bulgaria more successful

As you have already understood, you will be „a rare bird" when you are in the field with binoculars or a telescope in Bulgaria. You will be strange to the people there, but many things in this country will be strange to you too. That is why I have designed this guide in a way you to spend minimum efforts, to enjoy your birding and, of course, to see as many birds as possible. I hope that my 12-year long experience with tourists like you will be useful enough. What should you know in advance?

First of all, though the book gives very detailed descriptions, you definitely will be much more satisfied if you prefer to be in an organised tour. It can be organised only for you or for a group of birdwatchers. In any case, this is strongly recommendable rather than birdwatching on your own. There are many reasons for that, but the most serious among them are as follows:

– at the moment there is only one exact map of Bulgaria sold in the country, and this is a road map, but without all existing roads, with almost no details given about other geographical features (such as the relief, for example), and with a scale of 1:500 000;

– quite often there is no correspondence between the maps and the real elements of the territory itself;

– there are very few road signs showing the directions to the relevant villages and towns, especially outside the main roads, very few villages and towns have signs showing their names;

– almost none of the existing road signs is dubbed in Latin letters;

– relatively few people speaking a language other than Bulgarian, and people speaking foreign languages do not know much about nature around, as a rule;

— these factors are even more prominent in most of the areas interesting from a birding point of view, usually aside from the most urbanised areas.

– the names of many specific sites on the maps do not correspond to their local names known by the people there (this is especially widespread in the Eastern Rhodopi area);

Of course, do not think that Bulgaria is a wild area, where there is no place for strange foreigners who do not know Bulgarian. People in the country are very hospitable and kind, and be sure that very few people will refuse, for example, to share petrol (usually refusing any money) from their cars if your petrol is gone on a road. We suggest you our assistance in order you to spent your time in an optimal and pleasant possible way.

Besides our long experience and travelling throughout the country over the last 30 years, at many places the only way to find a specific place is, to ask some relevant local people. That is the reason to strongly recommend you to make birdwatching in Bulgaria in an organised way, preferably in a group. The BSPB Company „Neophron" Ltd., which is the main tool of the BSPB for self-supporting our conservation activities in the future, can help you in the best possible way in this respect. It can use the whole potential of the BSPB, including the large network of people throughout the country, the latest information on the birds, the most experienced bird guides in Bulgaria. When necessary, colleagues from „Neophron" Ltd. will put you in touch with the relevant local structures of the BSPB or with relevant people from the area, they can assist you, providing additional information or guidance on the place. For some sites this will help you to avoid areas sensitive from a point of view of private, border or military authorities. The Bulgarian Society for the Protection of Birds can facilitate you in getting in contact with „Neophron" Ltd., but you can call or write directly to them. If you decide to get in touch in advance with the BSPB Headquarters (BSPB HQ), you can find us as follows:

BSPB HQ
P.O.Box 114, BG-1172 Sofia, BULGARIA
for visit: Dianabad Housing Complex
              bl. 42, fl. 5, ap. 34
              phone/fax: +359 2 68 94 13
              phone: + 359 2 62 08 15

Neophron Ltd.
c/o BSPB Varna Branch
P.O.Box 492, BG-9000 Varna, BULGARIA
for visit: Varna Zoo
phone/fax: +359 52 30 25 36

In most cases, the descriptions of the sites are based on our previous experience and are designed in a way that most of the birds could be seen from the places outside or at the borders of the reserves and other protected areas. In these cases you need no permission. When you would like to enter a protected territory, you will need a written permission from the Ministry of Environment. To obtain it, you should write in advance to the following address:

Ministry of Environment
67, William Gladstone Str.
BG-1000 Sofia, BULGARIA
phone: +359 2 87 61 51
fax:+359 2 83 22 79

Upon request, „Neophron" Ltd. or the BSPB can provide you with recent information about the birds of the areas you want to visit, as well as with some other items which can make your birdwatching trip more fruitful. These can be maps, some Bulgarian books, brochures and other information materials, bird lists from previous trips, scientific publications on the relevant areas, etc. We can also arrange permissions for visiting the reserves or other protected areas from the relevant authorities.

Example ....

List of Bulgarian Birds

№	Scientific name	English vernacular name	Bulgarian vernacular name	Your language name
1.	*Gavia stellata*	Red-throated Diver	Червеногуш гмуркач	
2.	*Gavia arctica*	Black-throated Diver	Черногуш гмуркач	

You should take in consideration that at the moment there are no any special facilities for observing birds, as is common in many western countries. There are no observation hides or towers for watching birds in any of the Bulgarian reserves. The BSPB is constructing now the first two bird hides at Studen Kladenetz and at the Poda Reserve, but in general it will be necessary the birdwatchers to manage to see birds from open places. The descriptions in the book are based on our experience of watching birds under ordinary conditions. As mentioned above, this can be very successful, sometimes even just from the road. The way of watching birds at the relevant places is in conformity with the abilities of the ordinary birdwatchers, and it is possible to a large extend even for disabled people. So, do not hesitate to contact „Neophron" Ltd. or the BSPB which will make all to help you. The modest sums you will be charged with, they will be used for wildlife and nature which you will certainly find terrific.

BSPB will greatly appreciate receiving your bird list from our country. This will complete the data of the National Bank for Ornithological Information, it will enhance the monitoring of birds and especially the better planning of our conservation work. The monitoring of all Important Bird Areas (IBA) in Bulgaria is carried out by BSPB and your data about the specific sites can be of great help for the preservation of these places of European or Global Importance! We will be thankful to receive your data not only about IBAs, but also about other places, even not described in this book. Some of them may appear to be possible IBAs. To have compatible check-lists we would like to recommend you to fulfil the table at the end of the book as shown below, and to send a copy of it to either BSPB Head Quarter or to Neophron Ltd.

Thank you very much in advance!

.... *Example*

🖋 P l a c e 🦆 D a t e N u m b e r s ✦

	Silistra 14.06.97	Srebarna 14.06.97	Kalimok 14.06.97	Park in Ruse 15.06.97		Marsh near Sindel 20.06.97	Tzonevo 20.06.97							
		25	36		....		2							
					....									

How to use this book

I am sure that you already know this, but maybe some additional information will be of help the book to be easily used and to serve better to you. I would greatly appreciate any suggestions, remarks or additional information which could improve the use of the book or it itself.

The descriptions of the sites are arranged according to the regions, which makes their use easy, as the descriptions follow the sequence of the sites along the roads or in the relevant region.

It should be mentioned that the descriptions of the sites include mainly the species which, according to our experience, are of special interest to tourists from the countries of Western Europe. Of course, there will be exceptions as the birds interesting to a Swedish birdwatcher will not be the same as those a British will be interested in. Anyway, many other species occur at the described sites.

Sometimes you can see a phrase that „...almost all species of ... (terns, raptors, etc.) can be observed...". It is understood that this means „almost all European species".

All nature protected territories in the book are mentioned as „reserves". This is not completely correct, because, according to the Bulgarian legislation, there are several different categories of nature protected areas. Some of them do not correspond to the internationally recognised categories. But from a point of view of birdwatching, their differences do not make particular sense, that is why we have decided not to complicate the use of the book.

The important thing which must be taken in consideration, is that all bird species in Bulgaria, with the exception of 29 species, are protected by the Law. These species are as follows:

White-fronted Goose	*Anser albifrons*	....
Wigeon	*Anas penelope*	....
Mallard	*Anas platyrhynchos*	....
Pintail	*Anas acuta*	....
Shoveler	*Anas clypeata*	....

Teal	*Anas crecca*	....
Gargane	*Anas querquedula*	....
Tufted Duck	*Aythya fuligula*	....
Goldeneye	*Bucephala clangula*	....
Capercaillie	*Tetrao urogallus*	....
Chukar	*Alectoris chukar*	....
Rock Partridge	*Alectoris graeca*	....
Grey Partridge	*Perdix perdix*	....
Pheasant	*Phasianus colchicus*	....
Quail	*Coturnix coturnix*	....
Woodcock	*Scolopax rusticola*	....
Snipe	*Gallinago gallinago*	....
Herring Gull	*Larus argentatus*	....
Woodpigeon	*Columba palumbus*	....
Collared Dove	*Streptopelia decaocto*	....
Turtle Dove	*Streptopelia turtur*	....
Starling	*Sturnus vulgaris*	....
Jay	*Garrulus glandarius*	....
Magpie	*Pica pica*	....
Jackdaw	*Corvus monedula*	....
Hooded Crow	*Corvus corone cornix*	....
Rook	*Corvus frugilegus*	....
Tree Sparrow	*Passer montanus*	....
House Sparrow	*Passer domesticus*	....

(names in your language)

For all protected species it is forbidden, according to the Law, to catch (including for ringing or other scientific purposes), to kill, to stuff them regardless of their status and phase of development, without a written permission of the Ministry of Environment, to pursue, to disturb them during the breeding season, to destroy nests, to collect and destroy the eggs and youngs, to trade, exchange and export birds of protected species alive or stuffed, as well as their eggs and nests, without a written permission of the Ministry of Environment; zoos, museums and taxidermist laboratories to accept protected birds found killed, injured or dead. The Law allows exceptions to 3 of the protected species when specific conditions exist: the Cormorant *Phalacrocorax carbo* can be shot within fish farms when it damages them between 01 November and 31 January, the Rough-legged Buzzard *Buteo lagopus* can be shot between 01 December and 31 January when it damages game birds at the places of upfeeding and when there is snow cover, and the Bee-eater *Merops apiaster* during rains 150 m around bee-gardens and between 01 August and 30 September.

The site maps have been designed in a way to provide maximum information about how to get the best birding points and to orientate as easily as possible in the territory. They are based on precise topographic maps and each of them provides ample opportunity to quite exactly plan your approach and time in the territory thanks to the standard distance of 1 km shown on each of the maps. The main geographic names are given both in Bulgarian and English, which will make it possible to use the maps available in Bulgaria, and the existing road signs in Cyrillic. We have tried to put on maps as much and precise information as possible where exactly to see specific birds. It is to be understood that this information will not be 100% secure for the bird situation in different years. So, it will be better to consider the signs showing the places of occurrence of the birds on the maps as approximate, as places where the birds can be seen with the maximum probability. At the same time, the signs for the recommended observing points are quite stable and they have been identified during many years of birdwatching in the territory of the site. Most of them can be used by disabled people and it is easy to find them on the spot. The signs showing different elements of the territory are standard (or close to that) used usually on the maps. Nevertheless, it will be better to have their key.

Legend to the maps:

	settlement
	asphalt road, highway
	stone road
	cart-road, cart-track
	railway
	chair/cabin lift
	bridge
	tunnel
	marsh vegetation

meadows, pastures

 forests

 vineyards

 cliffs and other rocks, rocky and stony areas

 moraines

 loess or other soil walls

 periodically flooded islands

 sandy beach, sandy river bed

 sea cliffs, steep rocky or stony beach

 dykes

 canal

 dam

 cave

 carry

 monument

 tomb

 lighthouse

 cemetery

 border of a reserve

 recommendable observation place

Durankulak Lake (Дуранкулашко езеро)

Type: A fresh-water lake on the coastline of the Black Sea with rich marsh vegetation on the banks. Some small broad-leaved forests, lines of poplar and other trees around, and large agricultural fields, mixed at same places with wet meadows form its surroundings. From the Black Sea the lake is separated by a narrow sand beach. Small patches of land with steppe-like vegetation exist south of the lake. Several buildings of farms, a camping and archaeologists' camp are situated on the banks of the lake.

Location and strategy: The lake is located east of the village of Durankulak (Дуранкулак), near international road E87 (Konstantsa - Istambul). The area is excellent for birding all year round. In winter it is a roosting place for several thousands globally threatened RED-BREASTED GEESE. Like other sites along the Bulgarian part of the Black Sea coast, Durankulak Lake is very good for observing migrating SOARING BIRDS, as well as the other birds flying along the coast. In summer, the reedbeds of the lake are one of the very few places in Europe where it is possible to observe the PADDYFIELD WARBLER. In summer, the northeastern corner near the camping Cosmos (Къмпинг Космос) is a good place to start a short walk along the beach. Another good area during this season is the southwestern part of the lake, which can be reached turning to the east on an asphalt road 1 km south of the village. From the end of the asphalt it is possible to drive along a cart-road to archaeologists' camp. In winter, the best place to see GEESE taking off is the area to the east-

Acrocephalus agricola

southeast of the village of Durankulak (Дуранкулак), nearby the restaurant on the bank of the lake.

Birds: During the *breeding season,* it is possible to see the LITTLE GREBE, PYGMY CORMORANT (non-breeding on the lake), BITTERN and LITTLE BITTERN, PURPLE HERON, GREYLAG GOOSE, RUDDY SHELDUCK (some years), some species of DUCKS, including the RED-CRESTED POCHARD (some years), FERRUGINOUS DUCK, MARSH HARRIER (MONTAGU'S HARRIER breeds in the crops in the region), HOBBY and RED-FOOTED FALCON in the surroundings of the lake, CRAKES and RALES, STONE CURLEW (in the steppe area), COLLARED PRATINCOLE, LITTLE RINGED PLOVER (on the beach), LITTLE TERN, SCOPS and LITTLE OWL (in the town), KINGFISHER, BEE-EATER, ROLLER, HOOPOE, GREEN, SYRIAN and LESSER SPOTTED WOODPECKERS, CALANDRA LARK, TAWNY PIPIT, BLACK-HEADED YELLOW WAGTAIL (in the fields with crops), CIT-RINE WAGTAIL, SAVI'S, CETTI'S, GREAT REED, MARSH, REED, PADDYFIELD and OLIVACEOUS WARBLERS (on vegetation along

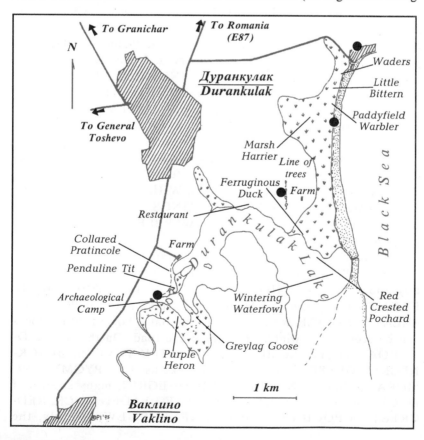

the banks and in areas with buildings), BEARDED and PENDULINE TITS, RED-BACKED SHRIKE, GOLDEN ORIOLE, ORTOLAN and BLACK-HEADED BUNTING, and others. Sometimes also some non-breeding SQUACCO HERONS, LITTLE and GREAT WHITE EGRETS, GLOSSY IBISES, BLACK-WINGED STILT, SANDWICH and CASPIAN TERNS, etc., can be seen.

Passage: The area is very rich in birds during the whole spring and autumn. RED-THROATED and BLACK-THROATED DIVERS can be observed on the sea. Almost all European species of GREBES use the lake and sea during this period. The PYGMY CORMORANT, WHITE and DALMATIAN PELICANS, WHITE and BLACK STORKS, almost all European species of HERONS, the GLOSSY IBIS and SPOONBILLS, many species of DUCKS, and almost all European species of RAPTORS fly through the area. Early in spring and late in autumn, flocks of COMMON CRANES can be seen. The shallow parts of the lake, especially in its northeastern end, attract many species of all groups of WADERS, including the BLACK-WINGED STILT, AVOCET, KENTISH PLOVER, RUFF, REDSHANK, SPOT-TED REDSHANK, GREENSHANK, WOOD SANDPIPER, MARSH SANDPIPER and in places with a richer vegetation, the WOODCOCK, SNIPE and JACK SNIPE can be observed. Some GULLS migrate through the area, including MEDITERRANEAN, SLENDER-BILLED, and LITTLE GULLS, as well as BLACK, WHITE-WINGED BLACK and WHISKERED TERNS. Flocks of BEE-EATERS are common on passage, as well as solitary ROLLERS and HOOPOES. Large numbers of SWALLOWS and MARTINS migrate over the lake, in marsh vegetation, the BLUETHROAT and many WARBLERS can be observed. The wet areas around the lake attract different species of PIPITS and WAGTAILS, in the places with bushes, WHINCHAT, STONECHAT, *Sylvia* WARBLERS, SHRIKES, BUNTINGS, on tree vegetation almost all European species of LEAF WARBLERS, FLYCATCHERS and other groups of birds can be seen.

Winter: The wintering birds of the Durankulak Lake are also very interesting. Without doubt, the most impressive are the GEESE. Usually about 160 000 WHITE-FRONTED, some LESSER WHITE-FRONTED and GREYLAG GEESE and up to 70 000 RED-BREASTED GEESE are wintering on the lake. Some feeding flocks can be seen in the winter crops near the road. On the sea, RED-THROATED and the BLACK-THROATED DIVERS, BLACK-NECKED GREBE can be seen, in the lake itself the PYGMY COR-MORANT, BITTERN, GREAT WHITE EGRET, many species of DUCKS (sometimes including the WHITE-HEADED DUCK, RED-CRESTED POCHARD, GOLDENEYE, SMEW). Rarely, the

WHITE-TAILED EAGLE can be seen too. In severe winters, GREAT and LITTLE BUSTARDS appear in the area. Rarely, even GREAT BLACK-HEADED GULL can be observed. The beach is a wintering site for the SANDERLING. Also many PASSERINES can be seen in winter time in the area.

Degree of difficulty: Almost all described places do not require any special effort and are relatively easy for observing birds by people of any degree of walking ability.

Facilities: *Fuel*: The nearest station is in Durankulak (Дуранкулак), 1-5 km from the lake.

Food: The village of Durankulak (Дуранкулак) offers some possibilities all year round, but they are quite limited. It is better to get supplied with food and drinks for the time you will be in the area. Some better opportunities exist at the cross-border point at 6 km north of the village, as well as in a small restaurant on the bank of the lake.

Accommodation: The nearest hotels are in the town of Shabla (Шабла), at 18 km from the place, where also some luxurious rooms in the Residence can be hired (a preliminary arrangement recommended). In summer, it is possible to stay in the campings around. Note that for the peak of the season (May - August), it is better to have reservation in advance.

Language: Mainly Bulgarian, but you can find people speaking English or other foreign languages at the hotels and campings.

Status: Reserve, Ramsar Site, IBA.

Permission: The banks of the lake are the limits of a reserve. No access to the wetland itself without a written permission of the Ministry of Environment, but there is free access to all described places around.

Recorder: BSPB HQ.

Shabla Lake (Шабленско езеро)

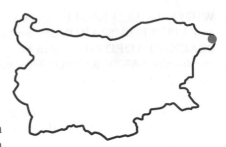

Type: A fresh-water lake on the coastline of the Black Sea, with rich marsh vegetation. There is a *Robinia pseudoacacia* forest near its northern part and a sand beach turns there into quite high dunes with specific vegetation, ending in the south near a small brackish-water lagoon called Shabla Tuzla (Шабленска тузла). From its western and southeastern sides, the lake is surrounded by agricultural fields, mixed at some places with wet meadows. Several buildings of the Government Residence Shabla (правителствена резиденция „Шабла") are situated on the bank of the lake and the Black Sea coastline. In the southern part of the area, the easternmost point of Bulgaria, Cape Shabla (нос Шабла) is situated. This is a place where the sand beach turns southward into sea cliffs with niches and caves. Some patches of a typical steppe vegetation exist in the area.

Location and strategy: The lake is situated about 5 km northeast of the town of Shabla (Шабла) which is on international road E87 (Konstantsa – Istambul). The Shabla Lake is very good for birding all year round. It is famous in that in winter it keeps almost all world population of the globally threatened **RED-BREASTED GOOSE** (up to 75% of all wild birds of the planet can be seen there in cold winters!). Like other sites along Black Sea coast, the Shabla Lake area is excellent for observing migrating **SOARING BIRDS**, as well as other

Branta ruficollis

birds following the coastline. During the breeding season, this is one of the very few places in Europe where it is possible to very easily observe the **PADDYFIELD WARBLER**. Dependent on the season, it is possible to make observations from several places. In summer, the northeastern corner and a short walk along the beach are the best to see many birds. In winter, the best place to see GEESE taking off (up to 300 000 birds! – one of the most impressive pictures of European Nature) is a field west of the lake itself. To reach the place, drive from the town of Shabla (Шабла) northward and, just before the bridge in the beginning of the nearest village of Ezeretz (Езерец), turn to the right (eastward) on a cart-truck and follow it to the fence of the Residence. Some 150 m further, from a higher field, the view is superb. It is possible also to turn to the right on the asphalt road leading to the farm (the turn is just near an old Thracean tomb) and to follow the road along the fence of the Residence northward to the highest part of the field, but this road is for a „Jeep" type of vehicle. The place southeast of the farm is very good for observing WADERS, HERONS and DUCKS. Another good place is the small watching tower on the roof of the Residence, for which it is necessary to drive eastward from the town of Shabla (Шабла), to turn northward after a small coniferous forest (straight on is the road to Cape Shabla (нос Шабла)), and you will reach a gate (access after a preliminary arrangement). For the small shallow lagoon Shabla Tuzla, the best is to turn eastward before the gate of the Residence and to turn to the right at the camping, and in its southern part you will be on the bank.

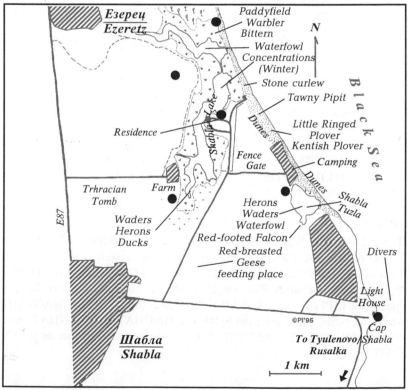

Birds: *Breeding birds* include RED-NECKED (some years) and LITTLE GREBES, SHAG (can be seen on the cliffs south of Cape Shabla), BITTERN and LITTLE BITTERN, PURPLE HERON, GREYLAG GOOSE (some years), SHELDUCK and RUDDY SHELDUCK (some years), some species of DUCKS, including FERRUGINOUS DUCK (some years), MARSH HARRIER (MONTAGU'S HARRIER breeds in the fields in the region, and RED-FOOTED FALCON – in tree lines there), CRAKES and RALES, the STONE-CURLEW (in the steppe area), BLACK-WINGED STILT (at Shabla Tuzla), LITTLE RINGED and KENTISH PLOVER (on the beach), LITTLE TERN, ROCK DOVE (on cliffs) SCOPS OWL, ROLLER (rarely), HOO-POE, GREEN, SYRIAN and LESSER SPOTTED WOODPECKERS, CALANDRA LARKS, TAWNY PIPIT (in dunes), BLACK-HEADED YEL-LOW WAGTAIL (in agricultural fields), ISABELLINE WHEATEAR, CETTI'S, GREAT REED, MARSH, REED, PADDYFIELD, BARRED and OLIVACEOUS WARBLERS (on vegetation along banks and in areas with buildings), BEARDED TIT, RED-BACKED SHRIKE, GOLDEN ORIOLE, ORTOLAN and BLACK-HEADED BUNTING, and others. During summer some other, non-breeding species can be seen, like the LITTLE WHITE EGRET, COLLARED PRATINCOLE, BLACK-WINGED STILT, SAND-WICH TERNS over the sea, etc.

Passage: The area is very rich in birds during the whole spring and autumn. Almost all European species of GREBES use the lake and the sea in this period. Despite the PYGMY CORMORANT, it is possible to observe large numbers of WHITE and DALMATIAN PELICANS, WHITE and BLACK STORKS, almost all European species of HERONS, flocks of GLOSSY IBIS and SPOONBILLS, many DUCK species and almost all European species of RAPTORS. Early in spring and late in autumn, flocks of COMMON CRANES fly over the beach. The wetlands (and especially the Shabla Tuzla) attract many species of all groups of WADERS, including the BLACK-WINGED STILT, AVOCET, KENTISH PLOVER, RUFF, REDS-HANK, SPOTTED REDSHANK, GREENSHANK, WOOD SANDPIPER, MARSH SANDPIPER, WOODCOCK, SNIPE and JACK SNIPE. Some GULLS can be seen in the area, including MEDITERRANEAN, SLEN-DER-BILLED, and LITTLE GULLS, as well as all species of MARSH TERNS: BLACK, WHITE-WINGED BLACK and WHISKERED TERNS. Flocks of BEE-EATERS are common on passage, as well as solitary ROLL-ERS and HOOPOES. Large numbers of SWALLOWS and MARTINS migrate over the wetlands. The wet areas around the lake support different species of PIPITS and WAGTAILS (including the CITRINE WAGTAIL), while the bushy parts are used by the WHINCHAT, STONECHAT, many species of WARBLERS and SHRIKES, on tree vegetation all species of FLY-CATCHERS can be observed.

Winter: The most interesting wintering birds in the area are GEESE. Usually about 100 000 WHITE-FRONTED, some LESSER WHITE-FRONTED and GREYLAG GEESE and, of course, between 15 000 and 70 000 RED-BREASTED GEESE are the birds coming every evening to the lake for roosting. During the day they get spread over winter crops in Dobrudzha, and some flocks can be seen just from the road on fields near the lake. On the lake and at Shabla Tuzla, it is possible to see RED-THROATED and BLACK-THROATED DIVERS, the BLACK-NECKED GREBE, PYGMY CORMORANT, BITTERN winter regularly and in good numbers there, the GREAT WHITE EGRET, WHOOPER SWAN, many species of DUCKS (including some DIVING DUCKS). Concentrated WATERFOWL attract sometimes the WHITE-TAILED EAGLE. In severe winters in the area, GREAT and LITTLE BUSTARDS can be seen. The Shabla Lake is one of the places where the GREAT BLACK-HEADED GULL has been observed. The beach is a wintering site for the SANDERLING. Many PASSERINES can also be seen in the winter time in the area.

Degree of difficulty: Almost all described points do not require any special effort and are relatively easy for observing birds by people of any degree of walking ability.

Facilities: *Fuel*: The nearest station is in Shabla (Шабла), about 5 km away from the site.

Food: The town of Shabla (Шабла) offers some possibilities all year round, there are small private restaurants there. It is possible to have arrangement with the Residence for having meal there too.

Accommodation: There are some hotels in the town of Shabla (Шабла) and luxurious rooms in the Residence (with preliminary arrangement). In summer, it is possible to stay in the campings around. Note that for the peak of the season (May — August) it is better to have reservation in advance.

Language: Mainly Bulgarian, but you can find people speaking English or other foreign languages at the hotels and campings.

Status: Reserve, Ramsar Site, IBA. Banks of the wetland are borders of the reserve.

Permission: No access to wetlands themselves, as well as to the territory of the Residence, but there is free access to all described places around.

Recorder: BSPB HQ.

Yailite
(Яйлите)

Type: A flat and open calcareous area, ending at the sea with 30 -50 m high cliffs, at some places forming several terraces. Small wetlands of different water salinity exist near the coastline. The most interesting is the marsh Taukliman (Тауклиман) near the Club Mediterranée village of Rusalka (Русалка). Stones and rocks of different sizes are scattered off the coast as islands of a miniature „archipelago". Many niches, holes and caves exist in cliffs. At some places in the flat area, on the top, there are also small hills of stones and ruins. The region around includes some of the last remains of steppe in Bulgaria. Agricultural lands and dry pastures together with some small villages and Rusalka complete the mosaic of habitats in the area.

Location and strategy: Yailite (Яйлите) is situated north of Cape Kaliakra (Нос Калиакра), about 80 km north of Varna (Варна) and about 56 km south of the cross-border point Durankulak (Дуранкулак), on international road E87. One of the best ways for birding there is to take a secondary road east of the town of Shabla (Шабла) and to drive southward to Kamen Briag (Камен бряг), from where to leave the road and to drive or walk on a cart-road southward to the archaeo-

Sturnus roseus

logical area. Next stop can be at the Rusalka village (Русалка), whence it is necessary to take another secondary road to Balgarevo (Българево), from which village it is possible to continue to Kaliakra Cape (Нос Калиакра) or to Varna (Варна). At many places it makes sense to stop near the road and watch interesting birds after a short walk.

Birds: *Breeding birds*: Yailite (Яйлите) is situated in the main area where the SHAG breeds in Bulgaria. The LITTLE BITTERN can be seen at the marsh

Taukliman. Sometimes the RUDDY SHELDUCK finds suitable niches
in cliffs for breeding. At some places the LONG-LEGGED BUZZARD
can be seen, usually over the plain. The RED-FOOTED FALCON
breeds in small colonies in tree lines or in groups of trees in the region. STONE-CURLEW is a regular breeder in the stony areas of the
plain. Among the FERAL PIGEONS which breed in cliffs, it is possible to see some quite clean specimens of the ROCK DOVE. The
EAGLE OWL breeds on cliffs, but it is difficult to get it. The LITTLE
OWL is common in villages. At some places, the ROLLER and HOO-
POE breed too. SHORT-TOED and CALANDRA LARKS, TAWNY
PIPIT, BLACK-EARED and PIED WHEATEARS, BLACK-HEADED
and CORN BUNTINGS are common breeders, usually in dry steppe
areas. In relevant years, the ROSE-COLOURED STARLING breeds
in this area, usually between stones gathered on small hills.

Passage: Like many similar places along the Black Sea coast,
Yailite (Яйлите) is excellent for observing birds migrating along the

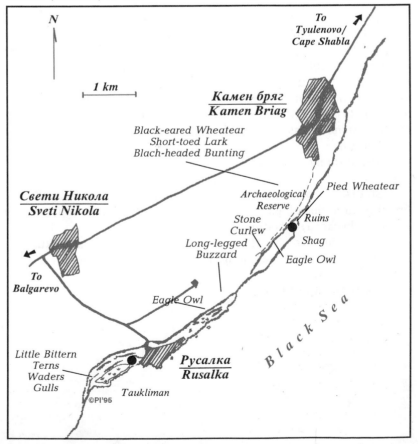

coastline. It is possible to observe on the sea the RED-THROATED and BLACK-THROATED DIVERS, almost all European species of GREBES, flocks of migrating WADERS, GULLS, SKUAS and TERNS. All species of SOARING BIRDS follow the coastline, including PELICANS, STORKS and RAPTORS, as well as non-soaring birds like HERONS, EGRETS and CRANES. Many species of WATERFOWL can be observed on the sea or on small wetlands, numerous PASSERINES of different species can also be seen.

Winter: Wintering birds include DIVERS, GREBES, CORMORANTS, some WATERFOWL, which can be seen on the sea or flying over the territory (the area is not far from the main wintering sites of the RED-BREASTED GOOSE).

Degree of difficulty: The area is very easy for birding for people with all degrees of walking abilities, usually the most interesting birds can be seen just from the road or after a short walk on a flat terrain.

Facilities: *Fuel*: The nearest possibilities to obtain it are in Kavarna (Каварна) and in Shabla (Шабла), both of which are at about 20 km.

Food: There are several opportunities to find food in Kavarna (Каварна), Shabla (Шабла), in the Club Mediterranée village Rusalka (Русалка) as well as in the small villages along the coast.

Accommodation: The nearest hotels are in the Club Mediterranée village of Rusalka (Русалка), in Kavarna (Каварна) and in Shabla (Шабла), but for a summer visit it is necessary to have reservation in advance.

Language: Some people in the area (at restaurants, resort places, etc.) speak foreign languages.

Status: Part of the area south of the village of Kamen Briag (Камен бряг) is an archaeological protected site, and the area southwest of Rusalka (Русалка) is Nature Reserve and IBA.

Permission: To visit the archaeological protected site, Rusalka, other settlements and sites along the road, no permission is necessary.

Recorder: BSPB HQ.

Cape Kaliakra
(Нос Калиакра)

Type: One of the most well-
known capes along the Bulgarian
Black Sea coast. This is a flat and open calcareous area, ending at the
sea with cliffs about 60 m high. Many niches, holes and caves make
the rocks quite attractive to birds. On the other hand, the location of
the cape is very much in favour of migrants. The region around is one
of the last remains of steppe in Bulgaria. A small valley with trees and
some tiny marshes exists north of Cape Kaliakra. There are several
operating and abandoned stone-pits on the plain around, which provide breeding opportunities for some specific birds. Agricultural lands
and some patches of pine plantations complete the mosaic of habitats.

Location and strategy: Cape Kaliakra (Нос Калиакра) is situated about 80 km north of Varna (Варна) and about 56 km south of
the cross-border point Durankulak (Дуранкулак) on international road
E87. One of the best places for birding here is east of Balgarevo
(Българево), where it is possible to stop near the road at the place
where there is a small hill with a topographic sign, and to have some
walk to the sea cliff on a cart-road to a stone-pit. The main place, of

Oenanthe pleschanka

course, is the cape itself, following an asphalt road. It is
possible to follow an asphalt
road to the small valley north
of the cape itself.

Birds: *Breeding birds*:
Kaliakra is part of the only area
in Bulgaria where the SHAG
breeds. The RUDDY SHEL-
DUCK finds suitable niches in
the cliffs for breeding in some
years. On the same cliffs,
LONG-LEGGED BUZZARD
breeds too, but birds can be
seen easily over the plain. Small

colonies of the RED-FOOTED FALCON exist in the tree lines in the region. Some years during the breeding season of other birds, ELEONORA'S FALCON can be seen over the cape or over the sea. The EAGLE OWL and some marshland birds can be spotted in the small valley north of the cape, the STONE-CURLEW can be observed on the stony plain, the ROLLER and HOOPOE breed there, too. The ALPINE SWIFT, SHORT-TOED and CALANDRA LARKS, TAWNY PIPIT, ISABELLINE, BLACK-EARED (in some years) and PIED WHEATEARS, BLACK-HEADED and CORN BUNTINGS are common breeders there. In some years, hundreds of ROSE-COLOURED STARLINGS can be seen.

Passage: Cape Kaliakra is excellent for observing almost all species of birds migrating along the Black Sea coast. It is possible to observe almost all European species of GREBES on the sea, as well as the YELKOUAN SHEARWATER, all species of soaring birds, including PELICANS, STORKS and RAPTORS, as well as such non-soaring ones as HERONS, EGRETS and CRANES. Many WATERFOWL, including the EIDER, many WADERS, GULLS, SKUAS and TERNS and, of course, large numbers of almost all migrating PASSERINES.

Winter: The wintering birds include DIVERS, GREBES, CORMORANTS, some WATERFOWL (the area is not far away from the main wintering sites of the RED-BREASTED GOOSE), etc.

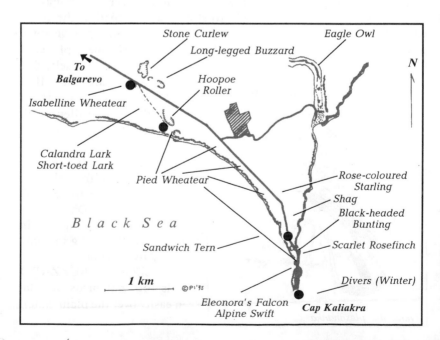

Degree of difficulty: The area is very easy for birding for people with all degrees of walking abilities, usually the most interesting birds can be seen just from the road or from the watching places of the cape.

Facilities: *Fuel*: The nearest possibility to obtain it is in Kavarna (Каварна), which is at about 15 km.

Food: There is a restaurant in the cave at the cape itself, quite a lot of opportunities to find food exist in the towns around: Kavarna (Каварна), Balchik (Балчик), Shabla (Шабла), etc.

Accommodation: The nearest hotels are in Kavarna (Каварна), but for a summer visit it is necessary to have reservation in advance.

Language: Some people in the area of the cape (at the restaurant, small museum, etc.) speak foreign languages.

Status: Part of the area around Kaliakra, including the cape, the territories to the west and north from it, as well as the aquatory are a reserve and IBA.

Permission: To visit the areas besides those described above, it is necessary to have a written permission from the Ministry of Environment.

Recorder: BSPB HQ.

Albena
(Албена)

Type: A summer resort on the northern Black Sea coast, where part of the former sandy beach and flooded forest are turned into a park-type woodland within which the buildings of the resort are situated, with some orchards, bushy and grassy areas. The resort touches the Reserve Baltata, which is one of the northernmost flooded forests in Europe. This forest is composed of old *Ulmus, Fraxinus, Quercus* and *Acer* trees with many lianas, bushes, flooded at least during one season per year. There are some small marshes.

Location and strategy: Albena (Албена) is situated about 35 km north of Varna (Варна), near international road E87. It is also on a major migration route (Via Pontica), following the Black Sea coastal line. This makes it a very good area for observing the migration of SOARING BIRDS and a very good starting point to many other birding sites around the northern Black Sea coast. The whole resort is good for the purpose of watching the migration, but probably the best site for this is the roof of the main Hotel Dobrudzha (Добруджа), from a small cafe bar up there. A good walking area is the southern part along the border of the reserve, but interesting birds can be seen virtually at any place of the resort.

Falco vespertinus

Birds: *Breeding birds*: the HOOPOE, GREY-HEADED (in the trees in the southern part of the resort), GREEN (in the resort itself), MIDDLE SPOTTED, SYRIAN and LESSER SPOTTED WOODPECKERS, OLIVACEOUS WARBLER (in the resort itself), LESSER WHITETHROAT, BARRED WARBLER (in the western part), RED-BACKED SHRIKE (common), GOLDEN ORIOLE (in the resort itself), CIRL and BLACK-HEADED

BUNTINGS, and others.

Passage: It is possible to see RED-THROATED and BLACK-THROATED DIVERS (in spring migrating even in the breeding plumage), as well as RED-NECKED and BLACK-NECKED GREBES on the sea. There is great variety of SOARING BIRDS over the resort: DALMATIAN and WHITE PELICANS, BLACK and WHITE STORKS, many species of RAPTORS (BLACK and RED KITES, EGYPTIAN VULTURES, MONTAGU'S, PALLID, HEN and MARSH HARRIERS, the SPARROWHAWK, GOSHAWK and LEVANT SPARROWHAWK, HONEY BUZZARD, BUZZARD and LONG-LEGGED BUZZARD, WHITE-TAILED, IMPERIAL, STEPPE, SPOTTED, LESSER SPOTTED, BOOTED and SHORT-TOED EAGLES, OSPREY, RED-FOOTED FALCON, KESTREL, HOBBY, LESSER KESTREL, PEREGRINE and SAKER. Flocks of NIGHT, SQUACCO and PURPLE HERONS, LITTLE EGRET, SPOONBILLS, GLOSSY IBISES, COMMON CRANES, AVOCETS, LAPWINGS, MEDITERRANEAN, SLENDER-BILLED and LITTLE GULLS, SANDWICH and COMMON TERNS, BEE-EATERS are also regular on migration. Other birds, such as the COMMON SANDPIPER, follow the coastline close to the beach or roost in the forest (WOODCOCK). Many species of LEAF WARBLERS, all species of FLYCATCHERS, etc. migrate at the same places.

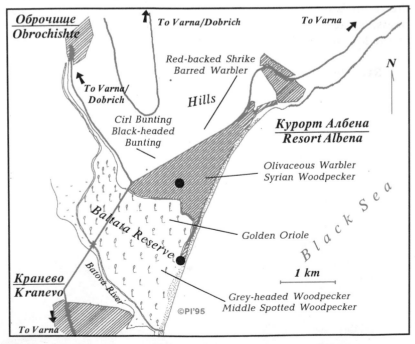

Winter: The most interesting birds during this season can be seen on the sea: RED-THROATED and BLACK-THROATED DIVERS, BLACK-NECKED GREBES, some DUCKS, RED-BREASTED MERGANSER, and others.

Degree of difficulty: Almost all birds mentioned in the description can be seen without special efforts by people with any degree of walking activity. Most birds can be observed just from the road.

Facilities: *Fuel*: The nearest possibilities to obtain it is the petrol station in the western part of the resort, near the crossroads to Varna (Варна) – Dobrich (Добрич).
Food: The resort provides many opportunities for different foods, including some food shops.
Accommodation: The resort offers different levels of accommodation opportunities. There are many small private hotels in all nearest towns and villages. Note that for the peak part of the season (May – August) it is better to have reservation in advance.
Language: Mainly Bulgarian, but you can find many people speaking English or other foreign languages at the resort.

Status: The forest in the southern part of the resort is a reserve.
Permission: Not required for the described places. The area of the resort is open to the public. There are many paths and asphalt roads. No access to the Baltata Reserve without a written permission by the Ministry of Environment.

Recorder: BSPB HQ.

Yatata
(Ятата)

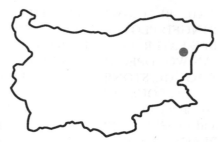

Type: A small marsh on the southern bank of Varna Lake, in its western part surrounded by wet and dry pastures, and from south and east by hills with exposed rocky faces. An asphalt road and a small valley with bushy vegetation and some trees separates Yatata from agricultural fields south of the marsh. From the brackish Varna Lake it is separated by a narrow open area and a dike. The small building of a water cleaning station is the only construction in the area.

Location and strategy: The marsh is situated about 2 km east of the town of Beloslav (Белослав) and at about 20 km from Varna (Варна), respectively from international road E87 (Konstantsa – Istambul). The area is excellent and easy for birding all year round. For a first observation place it is good to stop near the ship sign west of the village of Konstantinovo (Константиново) and to have a panorama view of the site. Another good place is also from the road on a hill south of the marsh. It is advisable to walk from there along the road to the south, afterwards on a cart-truck along a valley to the water cleaning station where it is also possible to have a good view of the marsh from a higher slope.

Tringa stagnatilis

Birds: During the *breeding season,* it is possible to see the LITTLE GREBE, PYGMY CORMORANT (non-breeding in the lake), LITTLE BITTERN, RUDDY SHELDUCK, FERRUGINOUS DUCK (some years), MARSH HARRIER, SHORT-TOED EAGLE (hunting over the dry areas around), WATER

RAIL, BLACK-WINGED STILT, AVOCET (some years), LITTLE RINGED PLOVER, LITTLE OWL (in the village of Konstantinovo), BEE-EATER, ROLLER, HOOPOE, WRYNECK, GREEN and SYRIAN WOODPECKERS, TAWNY PIPIT, BLACK-HEADED YELLOW WAGTAIL, STONECHAT, CETTI'S, GREAT REED, MARSH, REED, OLIVACEOUS and BARRED WARBLERS (the last two on vegetation along the valley), BEARDED TIT (some years), RED-BACKED and LESSER GREY SHRIKE, GOLDEN ORIOLE, ORTOLAN and BLACK-HEADED BUNTING, and others.

Passage: The area is rich in birds during the period of migration. Almost all European species of GREBES can be seen on the marsh or in the neighbouring part of Varna Lake. The PYGMY CORMORANT, BITTERN, almost all European species of HERONS, GLOSSY IBIS and SPOONBILL, many species of DUCKS, some RAPTORS cross the area at this time. Many species of all groups of WADERS, including the BLACK-WINGED STILT, AVOCET, RUFF, REDSHANK, SPOTTED REDSHANK, GREENSHANK, WOOD SANDPIPER, MARSH SANDPIPER and SNIPE can be seen. Some GULLS also visit the area, including MEDITERRANEAN, SLENDER-BILLED, and LITTLE GULLS, as well as LITTLE, BLACK, WHITE-WINGED BLACK and WHISKERED TERNS. BEE-EATERS are common on passage, as well as ROLLERS and HOOPOES. SWALLOWS and MARTINS migrate over the lake in large numbers, in vegetation many WARBLERS and other PASSERINES can be seen.

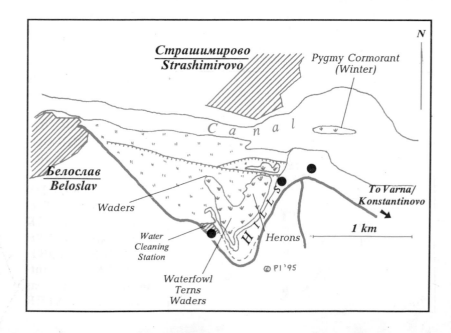

Winter: The wintering birds include RED-THROATED and BLACK-THROATED DIVERS, which can be seen sometimes on Varna Lake, LITTLE and BLACK-NECKED GREBES, PYGMY CORMORANT, BITTERN, GREAT WHITE EGRET, WHOOPER SWAN and many species of DUCKS (including the RED-CRESTED POCHARD, GOLDENEYE, SMEW, and others). Many PASSERINES can also be seen during the winter in the area.

Degree of difficulty: All described points with the exception of the walk along the valley do not require any special effort and are extremely easy for observing birds by people of any degree of walking ability.

Facilities: *Fuel*: The nearest station is in Beloslav (Белослав), 2 km from the site, others are in Varna (Варна), which is at about 20 km from the marsh.
   Food: The town of Beloslav (Белослав) offers some possibilities all year round, but they are not many. Much better opportunities exist in the town of Varna (Варна).
   Accommodation: The nearest hotels are in the town of Varna (Варна), which is at about 20 km from the marsh and where different levels of hotels exist. Note that for the peak of the season (May - August) it is better to have reservation in advance.
   Language: Mainly Bulgarian, but you can find people speaking English or other foreign languages in Varna.

Status: Reserve, IBA. The reserve territory is situated between the road and the bank of Varna Lake.
   Permission: No access to the reserve at places other than described without a written permission from the Ministry of Environment.

Recorder: BSPB HQ.

Kamchia
(Камчия)

Type: A flooded forest on
the Black Sea coast along the
banks of Kamchia River. Old ash, oak and other trees, abundant lianas and bushes hide many small ponds and other wetlands under the forest canopy. In the east, the forest reaches the sand dunes on the sea beach and the mouth of the river itself. Some small typical marshes exist at the border between the forest and the dunes. North of the mouth, there is a small summer resort which adds some park elements to the mosaic of habitats.

Location and strategy: Kamchia is situated about 30 km south of Varna (Варна), east of international road E87. There are mainly two ways for visiting the place. Following E87 from Varna (Варна) to Burgas (Бургас), after the village of Bliznatzi (Близнаци), turn to the left at the well signed crossroads to Kamchia Resort. Following the road, you will reach the summer resort at the river mouth proper. The second option is to travel to the village of Staro Oryakhovo (Старо Оряхово), to turn eastward in the village and to follow an asphalt road to Shkorpilovtzi (Шкорпиловци). After the village of Novo Oryakhovo (Ново Оряхово), the road enters the forest. Turn to the left (to the north) on a small asphalt road just before the Camping Izgrev (Къмпинг Изгрев), and after some 500 m you will be at the end of this road, whence you can start birdwatching in the area.

Phalacrocorax pygmeus

Birds: *Breeding birds:* On some of the marshes on the beach, the LITTLE BITTERN can be seen, in the same area the HOBBY hunts quite often, over the forest or at its edge the BLACK STORK, LESSER SPOTTED

EAGLE, GOSHAWK can be observed, the LITTLE RINGED PLO-
VER breeds on the beach, the SCOPS OWL can be heard in the night,
as well as NIGHTJAR. The area is good for the HOOPOE. WRY-
NECK, BLACK, GREY-HEADED, GREEN, MIDDLE SPOTTED,
GREAT SPOTTED and LESSER SPOTTED WOODPECKERS which
are breeders there. On sand dunes, the TAWNY PIPIT can be seen, in
the bushes in the area the BARRED WARBLER breeds. One of the
highlights there is the SEMI-COLLARED FLYCATCHER, although it
can be seen much easier at the neighbouring site Goritza (Горица)
(see the relevant pages). This is also one of the very few places in
Bulgaria, where the ICTERINE WARBLER can be seen during the
breeding season.

Passage: Kamchia like all similar sites along the Bulgarian Black
Sea coast, is famous for the possibility to see a great variety of migrants: from DIVERS and GREBES on the sea, all soaring species,
including PELICANS, STORKS and RAPTORS, as well as such non-
soaring birds as HERONS, EGRETS and CRANES, in the air, many
WADERS, GULLS and TERNS along the coastline, the KINGFISHER
can be observed more often than during the breeding season and, of
course, large numbers of forest migrants, including all European species of FLYCATCHERS.

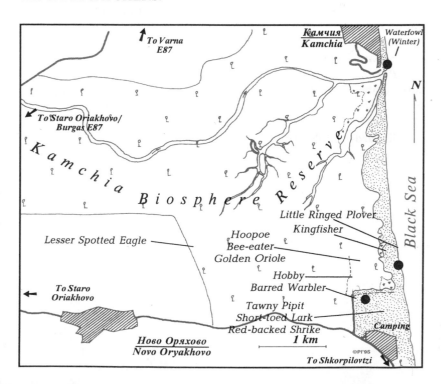

Winter: The best for a winter visit is the area around the river mouth itself. DIVERS, GREBES, CORMORANTS, some WATER-FOWL, etc.

Degree of difficulty: Both described ways for birding in the area are very easy for people with all degrees of walking abilities. There are many possibilities for short walks around, but the most interesting birds can be seen just from the road.

Facilities: *Fuel*: The nearest possibility to obtain it is in Staro Oryakhovo (Старо Оряхово), which is at 10 - 15 km from the birding places.
Food: There are some opportunities to obtain food in the villages around, but it is better to get supplied in advance with food and drinks for a stay at the site, especially out of the resort season.
Accommodation: The nearest hotels are in the Kamchia resort, which operate mainly in the summer time. It is better to have reservation in advance there. In summer, another opportunity is Camping Izgrev (Къмпинг Изгрев) and the hotels in Shkorpilovtzi (Шкорпиловци).
Language: Almost no people speaking English or other foreign languages in the villages around. Most of the people in the resort and camping speak foreign languages.

Status: Kamchia is a biosphere reserve and IBA.
Permission: To enter the Reserve at any place, besides those described above, it is necessary to have a written permission from Ministry of Environment.

Recorder: BSPB HQ.

Goritza Forest (гората до Горица)

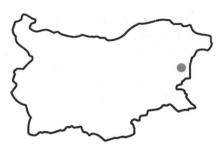

Type: A broad-leaved forest with rich bushy vegetation, but of varying densities, near international road E87 and near a small road-by restaurant.

Location and strategy: The place is situated just near international road E87, about 1 km northwest of the village of Goritza (Горица), 46 km south of Varna (Варна). To observe birds, it is enough to simply leave the car near the restaurant and to take a short walk in the forest.

Birds: *Breeding birds*: Typical forest birds and species connected with human settlements: the SPARROWHAWK, TAWNY OWL, NIGHTJAR, BLACK, GREEN, MIDDLE SPOTTED WOODPECKERS, WOODLARK, TREE PIPIT, REDSTART, WOOD WARBLER, SEMI-COLLARED FLYCATCHER, SOMBRE TIT, SHORT-TOED TREECREEPER, GOLDEN ORIOLE, HAWFINCH, YELLOWHAMMER, and others.
Passage: Almost all European species of woodland PASSERINES can be observed. Many SOARING BIRDS can be seen flying relatively low over the forest, even such species as WHITE PELICANS, BLACK STORKS, RAPTORS.

Ficedula semitorquata

Winter: Several species of WOODPECKERS and some PASSERINES can be seen in the forest.

Degree of difficulty: Most of the birds can be seen during a very easy walk on an almost flat terrain, so the place is good for people with any degree of walking abilities.

Facilities: *Fuel*: The nearest possibilities to obtain it are in Byala (Бяла), 7 km and in Staro Oryakhovo (Старо Оряхово), 14 km.

Food: It is possible to have meal in a small restaurant on the spot, as well as in small coffee bars there.

Accommodation: The nearest hotels are in the towns of Byala (Бяла), 7 km, and of Obzor (Обзор), 14 km, but beyond the high season the opportunities are restricted.

Language: There are some people speaking English or other foreign languages in the restaurant and in the mentioned towns.

Status: No special statute.

Permission: Not required.

Recorder: BSPB HQ.

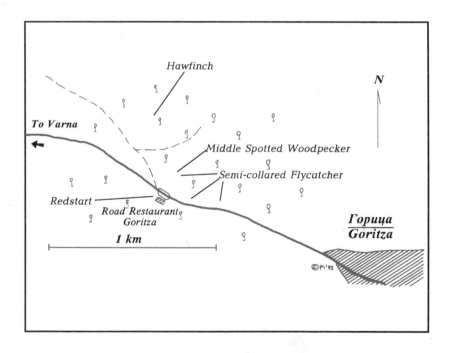

Cape Emine
(Нос Емине)

Type: One of the most well-known capes along the Bulgarian Black Sea coast, the easternmost point of the Balkan Range. At this place the mountain is lower and the hills end at the sea with stony and shingly, almost vertical walls, 20 to 50 m high. The height and location of the cape is very much of favour for migrants. The region around is hilly and quite well forested. Small valleys with trees and bushes go down to the sea between open bushy slopes. Part of the site is of a park type, with old trees, mixed with grassy areas with bushes. The small village of Emona (Емона) and a military area are the only built-up zones.

Location and strategy: Cape Emine (Нос Емине) is situated about 75 km north of Burgas (Бургас), about 82 km south of Varna (Варна) and at 14 km from international road E87. Turn toward the sea at the road sign to Irakli (Иракли), drive some 2 km and turn to the south (before reaching the beach itself) along an asphalt road (which in its higher part becomes cart-road), and follow it to the cape itself. It is possible to leave the car near the gate of the military area and to walk toward a light house. To the west there is a small valley which can be checked for the OLIVE-TREE WARBLER, and from it you can cross the road and approach the eastern side of the beach, where FINSCH'S WHEATEAR can be seen. The same place is excellent for sea watching and observing migrating RAPTORS.

Birds: *Breeding birds*: During the breeding season in the region of Emine, it is possible to see the YELKOUAN SHEARWATER (over the sea), GOSHAWK, HONEY BUZZARD, LESSER SPOTTED EAGLE, HOBBY (in

Hippolais olivetorum

the forested area), LITTLE RINGED PLOVER (on the beach), SCOPS
and LITTLE OWLS, NIGHTJAR, HOOPOE, WRYNECK, GREEN
and SYRIAN WOODPECKERS, TAWNY PIPIT, STONECHAT,
BLACK-EARED and FINSCH'S WHEATEARS, ROCK and BLUE
ROCK THRUSHES, OLIVE-TREE and OLIVACEOUS WARBLERS,
BARRED WARBLER, SOMBRE TIT, CIRL, ORTOLAN, BLACK-
HEADED and CORN BUNTINGS, and others. Sometimes non-breeding MEDITERRANEAN GULLS, SANDWICH TERNS and other
species can be seen in the area.

Passage: Cape Emine is excellent for observing almost all species
of birds migrating along the Black Sea coast. On the sea it is possible
to see both species of DIVERS and almost all European species of

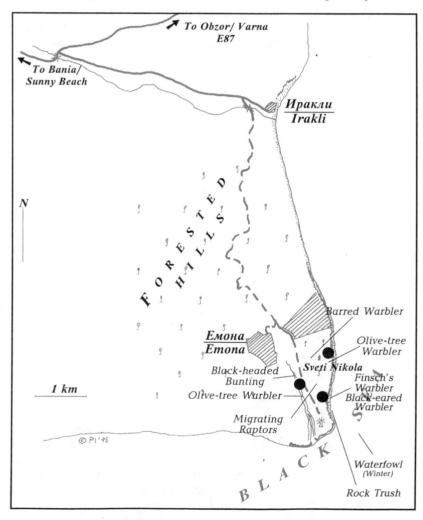

GREBES, as well as the YELKOUAN SHEARWATER, all species of soaring birds fly very low over this area, including PELICANS, STORKS and RAPTORS, the non-soaring species as HERONS, EGRETS and CRANES can also be seen from the cape. Many WATERFOWL, WADERS, GULLS, SKUAS and TERNS and, of course, large numbers of almost all migrating PASSERINES are possible to be observed.

Winter: The wintering birds include DIVERS, GREBES, CORMORANTS, some WATERFOWL, PASSERINES, etc.

Degree of difficulty: Birding in the area is very easy for people with any degree of walking ability, usually the most interesting birds can be seen just from the road or during a short walk on an almost flat terrain.

Facilities: *Fuel*: The nearest possibility to obtain it is in Obzor (Обзор), which is at about 22 km.

Food: There are almost no possibilities to obtain food in the area, so it is better to get supplied with food and drinks for the whole stay. A lot of opportunities to have meal exist during the resort season in the towns around: Obzor (Обзор), Sunny Beach (Слънчев бряг), etc.

Accommodation: The nearest hotels are in Obzor (Обзор), 22 km and in Sunny Beach (Слънчев бряг), 40 km, but for a summer visit it is necessary to have reservation in advance.

Language: Almost no people speaking English or other foreign languages in the area of the cape.

Status: IBA.
Permission: Not required.
Recorder: BSPB HQ.

Sunny Beach
(Слънчев бряг)

Type: A summer resort on the Black Sea coast, where part of the former sandy beach is turned into a park-type woodland within which the buildings of the resort are situated, with many bushes and grass vegetation of complex structure. Two small rivers with marsh vegetation, a large pool in place of a former sand pit in the southern part of the resort, wet meadows near its northwestern corner, some more typical woodland areas and some remains of sand dunes enrich the habitats of the site.

Location and strategy: Sunny Beach (Слънчев бряг) is situated about 40 km north of Burgas (Бургас) and only 1 km away from Nesebar (Несебър) near international road E87. Its position at a large bay of the Black Sea, the vicinity of the Balkan Range and the mosaic of different habitats make it a very good area for birding and a starting point to many other birding sites along the Black Sea coast. The best areas are in its northern part and along the river in its southern part, as well as the water pool, but interesting birds can be seen virtually at any place of the resort. To reach the wet meadows in the northwestern part, it is possible to walk along the asphalt road leading to the village of Kosharitza (Кошарица).

Upupa epops

Birds: *Breeding birds*: The LITTLE GREBE (on the river in some years), LITTLE BITTERN (within reedbeds of the river), KESTREL (on buildings in the northern part), QUAIL (can be heard calling in crops west of the resort), CORNCRAKE (can be heard in wet meadows), LITTLE RINGED PLOVER (on the beach), LITTLE TERN (near the mouth of the river in the southern part), SCOPS OWL, KINGFISHER, HOOPOE (sometimes even in holes of the buildings), GREY-HEADED (in trees in the

northern part of the resort), GREEN (in the resort itself), MIDDLE SPOT-
TED, SYRIAN, GREAT SPOTTED and LESSER SPOTTED WOODPECK-
ERS, RED-RUMPED SWALLOW (under the bridge on the road to
Kosharitza (Кошарица), CETTI'S, GREAT REED, MARSH and REED
WARBLERS (in reed and other vegetation along the river), OLIVACEOUS
WARBLER (very numerous in the resort itself), LESSER WHITETHROAT,
BARRED WARBLER (both in the northern part), RED-BACKED SHRIKE
(common), GOLDEN ORIOLE (in the resort itself), SPANISH SPARROWS
(inside letters of the signs on hotels), CIRL and BLACK-HEADED BUN-
TINGS, and others.

Passage: Solitary RED-THROATED and BLACK-THROATED
DIVERS, groups of RED-NECKED and BLACK-NECKED GREBES

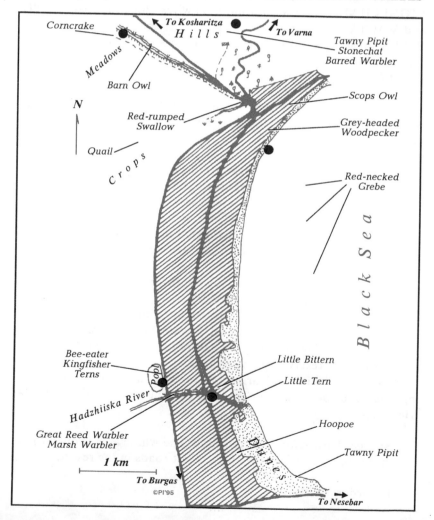

can often be seen on the sea, sometimes YELKOUAN SHEARWA-
TERS cross the bay. From among the SOARING BIRDS, DALMA-
TIAN and WHITE PELICANS, BLACK and WHITE STORKS, many
species of RAPTORS can be observed over the resort. Flocks of NIGHT,
SQUACCO and PURPLE HERONS, LITTLE EGRET, SPOON-
BILLS, GLOSSY IBISES, COMMON CRANES, AVOCETS, LAP-
WINGS, MEDITERRANEAN GULLS, SANDWICH and COMMON
TERNS, BEE-EATERS are also regular on migration. On the pool of
the sand pit, BLACK, WHITE-WINGED BLACK and WHISKERED
TERNS can be seen regularly on migration. Other birds as COMMON
SANDPIPER stick to the beach or to the more quiet parts of the for-
ests around, like the WOODCOCK. ROLLERS, WHINCHATS,
STONECHATS can be seen usually on wires along the road, PIPITS
and WAGTAILS are in open fields. Several species of LEAF WAR-
BLERS, all species of FLYCATCHERS cross the resort over its main
vegetation.

Winter: The most interesting birds during this season can be seen
on the sea: RED-THROATED and BLACK-THROATED DIVERS,
BLACK-NECKED GREBES, some WATERFOWL (most often the
MUTE SWAN, but also some DUCKS, the RED-BREASTED MER-
GANSER).

Degree of difficulty: Almost all birds mentioned in the description can be seen without special effort and by people with any degree
of walking activity. Most birds can be seen just from the road/street.

Facilities: *Fuel*: The nearest possibilities to obtain it is a petrol
station in the southern part of the resort, near the crossroads to Nesebar
(Несебър).

Food: The resort provides many opportunities for different food,
including a food shop in the center.

Accommodation: The resort offers different levels of accommodation opportunities. Many small private hotels exist in Nesebar
(Несебър). Note that for the peak part of the season (May - August) it
is better to have reservation in advance.

Language: Mainly Bulgarian, but you can find many people speaking English or other foreign languages at the resort and in Nesebar
(Несебър).

Status: *Permission*: Not required. The whole area is open to the
public. There are many paths and asphalt roads in the resort.

Recorder: BSPB HQ.

Aheloi
(Ахелой)

Type: The lower flow of a
small river before its mouth into
the Black Sea, where small dams provide a marshland type of the area.
Beside marsh vegetation, some trees, bushes and grasses form quite
dense belts along the banks.

Location and strategy: Aheloi River (река Ахелой) is situated at
the southern end of the village of Aheloi (Ахелой), 7 km south of
Sunny Beach (Слънчев бряг) and 29 km north of Burgas (Бургас), on
international road E87. To observe birds, it is enough to simply stop
near the road.

Birds: *Breeding birds*: The most common birds which can be ob-
served during the breeding season are the LITTLE GREBE, PYGMY
CORMORANT (not breeding there), LITTLE BITTERN,
SQUACCO HERON (non breeding), LITTLE EGRET (non breeding),
SPOTTED CRAKE, WATER RAIL, BLACK-WINGED STILT (not
breeding), LITTLE TERN, KINGFISHER, SYRIAN WOODPECKER,
GREAT REED and REED WARBLERS, OLIVACEOUS WARBLER,
and others.

Sterna albifrons

Passage: Some species of
GREBES, almost all European
species of HERONS and
EGRETS, some WADERS, the
MARSH TERNS, many species of
PASSERINES can be observed.
Many SOARING BIRDS can be
seen flying over the coastline.
Winter: The site is located
between the most important win-
tering places of the PYGMY
CORMORANT along the Bulgar-
ian part of the Black Sea coast.

Degree of difficulty: Almost
all birds can be seen just from the
road, so the place is good for

people with any degree of walking abilities. There are possibilities for some short walks along the bank of the river.

Facilities: *Fuel*: The nearest possibilities to obtain it are in Sunny Beach (Слънчев бряг), 7 km and in Pomorie (Поморие), 8 km.

Food: Many possibilities exist, especially in the resort season, in the village of Aheloi, in Sunny Beach and in Pomorie.

Accommodation: There are many hotels of different levels, especially in the resort season, in the village of Aheloi, in Sunny Beach, in Pomorie and Burgas.

Language: There are some people speaking English or other foreign languages, even in the village of Aheloi.

Status: No special statute.
Permission: Not required.

Recorder: BSPB HQ.

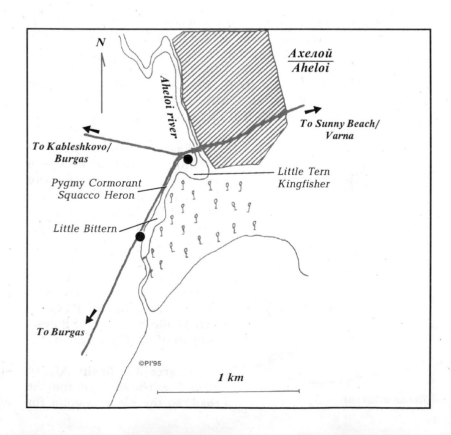

Pomorie Lake
(Поморийско
езеро)

Type: A hypersaline shallow
lake - a coastal lagoon, about 90% of which is used for salt production in a traditional primitive way. This fact together with the position
of the lake on a very busy migratory route along the Black Sea coast
(Via Pontica) favour large numbers of birds. There are pools with salt
water of different degrees of salinity, as well as fresh water bodies.
Some small marshes with rich vegetation exist in the southern part of
the lake. Vineyards and agricultural fields lie west of the lake, and a
narrow dike separates it from a sandy sea beach. In the very south, the
lake reaches an urban area of the town of Pomorie (Поморие).

Location and strategy: The lake is situated north of the town of
Pomorie (Поморие). In the southern part, the Pomorie Lake remains
east of international road E87 and in the northern part there are pools
on both sides of the road. Being situated on the coastline, this place is
extremely interesting from point of view of observing migrating SOAR-
ING BIRDS. The easiest way is to stop near the road and to observe
from there. Any place along the lake is good, especially in the northern part. There is a short local road to the buildings of the salt company, which can be used to reach places more close to the main part
of the lake and to be closer to the sea. From the town of Pomorie
(Поморие), it is possible to reach the dike between the sea beach and
the lake (drive to the north toward the places for taking medical mud

Recurvirostra avocetta

(пунктовете за меди-
цинска кал) and you will
reach the beginning of
the dike. Leave the car
there and walk on the
dike (good during the
first half of the day and
in passage as well as in
winter time).
    Birds: More than
215 species of birds have
been recorded in Pomo-

rie Lake. It is rich in birds (in terms of both numbers and interesting species) all year round. ***Breeding birds*** include the LITTLE GREBE, LITTLE BITTERN, GADWALL, MARSH HARRIER, CRAKES and RALES (all in marshy areas), the BLACK-WINGED STILT, AVOCET (on the banks of pools, some can be seen from very close distance from the road itself), the REDSHANK, COLLARED PRATINCOLE (in some years using dry pastures west of the lake), KENTISH PLOVER, COMMON and LITTLE TERNS, the KINGFISHER, TAWNY PIPIT (in dry surroundings of the lake), BLACK-HEADED YELLOW WAGTAIL (in agricultural fields), CETTI'S, GREAT REED, MARSH, REED, OLIVACEOUS (on tree and bushy vegetation near the lake) WARBLERS, the BEARDED TIT, RED-BACKED SHRIKE, BLACK-HEADED BUNTING, and others. During summer, some other non-breeding species can be seen, such as the PYGMY CORMORANT,

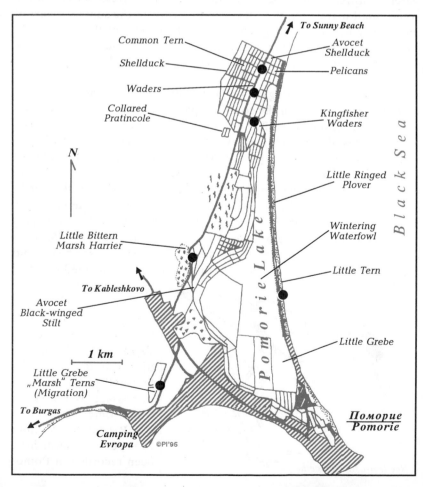

LITTLE EGRET, SPOONBILL, GLOSSY IBIS, MEDITERRANEAN and SLENDER-BILLED GULLS, the GULL-BILLED TERN, and others.

Passage: Like other sites along the Black Sea coast, the area is extremely interesting for birding in spring and autumn in Bulgaria. Almost all European species of GREBES can be seen on the lake or on the sea during this period. This is a regular route for flocks of WHITE and DALMATIAN PELICANS (some stop for roosting), WHITE and BLACK STORKS, almost all European species of HERONS, GLOSSY IBISES and SPOONBILLS, many species of DUCKS and RAPTORS, COMMON CRANES. The site is of great interest from a point of view of almost all species of European WADERS. Quite abundant are various species of STINTS and SANDPIPERS (including the BROAD-BILLED and the WOOD SANDPIPERS), less numerous are other species, such as GOLDEN and GREY PLOVERS, CURLEWS, BLACK-TAILED and BAR-TAILED GODWITS, SPOTTED REDSHANKS, GREENSHANKS, MARSH SANDPIPERS, SNIPES and JACK SNIPES, RED-NECKED PHALAROPES. Some solitary TURNSTONES, WHIMBRELS, GREAT SNIPES can also be seen. The place is very good for many species of GULLS - MEDITERRANEAN, SLENDER-BILLED and LITTLE GULLS are abundant, as well as MARSH TERNS: BLACK, WHITE-WINGED BLACK and WHISKERED TERNS. BEE-EATERS' flocks are also frequent over the area, as well as solitary ROLLERS and HOOPOES. This can be said for many of the European LARKS, SWALLOWS and MARTINS, PIPITS. It is not so easy to observe the BLUETHROAT, nor *Locustella* and *Acrocephalus* WARBLERS, but they migrate in large numbers too.

Winter: The wintering birds of Pomorie Lake include solitary RED-THROATED and BLACK-THROATED DIVERS, almost all species of GREBES, lots of PYGMY CORMORANTS, DALMATIAN PELICANS, the BITTERN, GREAT WHITE EGRET, many species of DUCKS (including the SCAUP and some other DIVING DUCKS); sometimes on the sea, COMMON and VELVET SCOTTERS can be seen, the SANDERLING, restricted to the beach, BARN and SHORT-EARED OWLS, some PASSERINES.

Degree of difficulty: All described places require no special effort and are very easy for observing birds by people of any degree of walking ability.

Facilities: *Fuel*: The nearest station is in Pomorie (Поморие).

Food: Pomorie (Поморие) provides many opportunities for different foods.

Accommodation: The nearest hotels are in Pomorie (Поморие), where there are different accommodation opportunities (including small private hotels). Note that for the peak of the season (May - August) it is better to have reservation in advance.

Language: Mainly Bulgarian, but you can find people speaking English or other foreign languages at Pomorie (Поморие).

Status: Reserve, IBA. Banks of the wetland are borders of a protected area.

Permission: As a reserve, entering Pomorie Lake at any place other than described above needs a written permission from the Ministry of Environment.

Recorder: BSPB HQ.

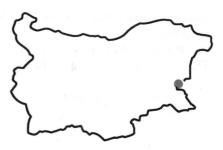

Camping Evropa marsh (блатото до къмпинг Европа)

Type: A small fresh-water marsh with low water vegetation on the Black Sea coast near international road E87. A sand beach with man-made stone breakwater and the road divide it from the sea. From the west, agricultural fields surround the marsh. A water cleaning station discharges water into the marsh. A small camping site is situated north of the marsh.

Location and strategy: The camping Evropa marsh (блатото до къмпинг Европа) is situated 7 km west of the town of Pomorie (Поморие) and 14 km north of Burgas (Бургас), on international road E87. To observe birds, it is enough to simply stop near the road.

Birds: *Breeding birds*: The most common birds which can be seen during the breeding season are the LITTLE GREBE, LITTLE BITTERN (non-breeding), SQUACCO HERON (non-breeding), LITTLE EGRET (non-breeding), GARGANEY (non-breeding), BLACK-WINGED STILT the (main breeding species), AVOCET (non-breeding), BLACK-HEADED YELLOW WAGTAIL, MARSH WARBLER, OLIVACEOUS WARBLER, and others.

Passage: Almost all European species of HERONS and EGRETS, some of the European DUCKS (including the GADWALL), some WADERS (including the REDSHANK, SPOTTED REDSHANK, GREENSHANK, WOOD SANDPIPER and MARSH SANDPIPER, SNIPE and JACK SNIPE), BLACK, WHITE-WINGED BLACK and WHISKERED TERNS, some PASSERINES

Himantopus himantopus

can be observed. Many SOARING BIRDS can be seen flying over the coastline.

Winter: The GREEN SANDPIPER in the marsh itself, some WATERFOWL can be seen on the sea.

Degree of difficulty: Almost all birds can be spotted just from the road, so the place is good for people with any degree of walking abilities.

Facilities: *Fuel*: The nearest possibilities to obtain it are in Pomorie (Поморие), 7 km and in Burgas (Бургас), 14 km.

Food: Many possibilities exist, especially in the resort season, in all campings and towns along the coast.

Accommodation: Many hotels of different levels exist, especially in the resort season, in the towns Pomorie and Burgas, in the campings and at Sunny Beach.

Language: There are some people speaking English or other foreign languages in the campings and settlements along the coast.

Status: No special statute.
Permission: Not required.

Recorder: BSPB HQ.

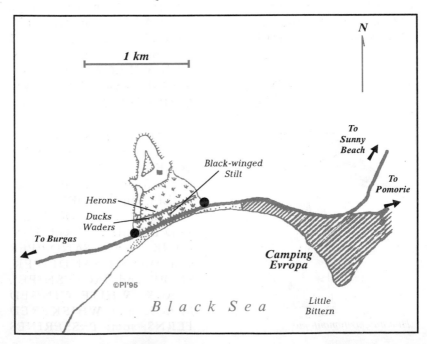

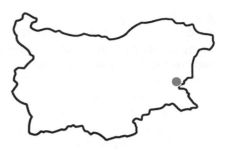

Atanasovo Lake (Атанасовско езеро)

Type: A hypersaline shallow lake – a coastal lagoon, most of the territory of which is used for salt production in a traditional primitive way. This provides excellent conditions for large numbers of birds specific for lagoons and estuaries. The pools with salt water of different degree of salinity are surrounded by a fresh-water canal and some fresh or brackish water small marshes covered with rich vegetation of different types. Dry pastures, wet meadows and agricultural fields exist around the northern half of the lake, and the sea shore and urban area surround its southern and southeastern parts.

Location and strategy: The lake is situated near the town of Burgas (Бургас), which lies at the westernmost corner of the Black Sea coast. For migrating SOARING BIRDS, this is a typical „bottle-neck" site, where (especially in autumn) migrating birds get concentrated in a very narrow front. The easiest way to reach the southern side of the lake is to go to the park area of the town of Burgas (Бургас) near the Hotel-Park (Хотел Парк) and to observe birds from there. Another way is to follow an old road (asphalt) along the sea shore, but it can be used up to the barrier near the salt factory offices. This way is good for the first half of the day because the light will be from your back side.

A third (and probably the best from a point of view of seeing almost all interesting birds) approach to the site is an asphalt road on the eastern side of the northern part of the lake. This is the road to the mines Cherno More (Мини Черно море) and Kableshkovo (Каблешково). Just before the end of the fence of a small air field (you will see small air-

Glareola pratincola

crafts before it) east of the road, turn to the left and by an asphalt road you can reach a rail near the bank of the lake. Walk northward along a cart-road some one hundred meters, and after a small pond turn to the west toward the bank of the lake. Cross the small sluce, and you will be on a dyke, which is near a shallow water pond. This is the place from which most of the birds can be seen. After that go back to the pond and turn left (to the north), pass across a small bridge and follow the land road between the reedbeds up to the open fields east of the lake. If your time for Atanasovo Lake is limited, a very good place is the road separating the lake into the northern and southern parts. According to the part of the day you want to watch birds, choose its

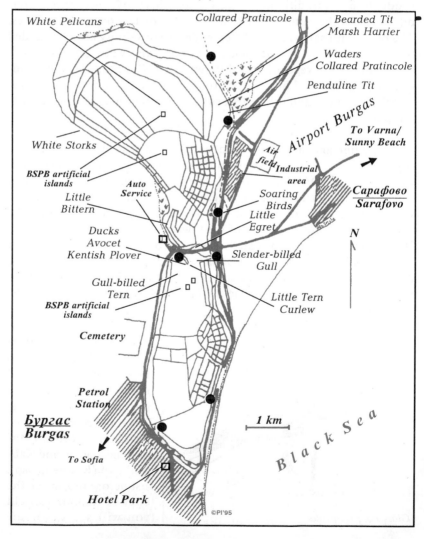

eastern or western part. For a more stationary observation of the migration of SOARING BIRDS, the best place is the dyke near the group of small buildings at the southeastern corner of the northern part of the lake.

Birds: More than 250 species of birds have been recorded in Atanasovo Lake. It is rich in birds (both in numbers and in interesting species) all year round. *Breeding birds* include the LITTLE BITTERN, PURPLE HERON, MARSH HARRIER, CRAKES AND RALES, BLACK-WINGED STIILT, AVOCET, COLLARED PRATINCOLE, KENTISH PLOVER, MEDITERRANEAN GULL, GULL-BILLED, SANDWICH and LITTLE TERNS, KINGFISHER, TAWNY PIPIT, BLACK-HEADED YELLOW WAGTAIL, SAVI'S, CETTI'S, GREAT REED, MARSH, REED, OLIVACEOUS and BARRED WARBLERS, BEARDED and PENDULINE TITS, RED-BACKED SHRIKE, BLACK-HEADED BUNTING, and others. During summer some other, non-breeding species can be seen, such as the PYGMY CORMORANT, LITTLE EGRET, SPOONBILL, GLOSSY IBIS, SLENDER-BILLED GULL, CASPIAN TERN, etc. In the years with higher numbers, flocks of ROSE-COLOURED STARLINGS can be observed there.

Passage: The area is one of the best for birding in spring and autumn in Bulgaria. Almost all European species of GREBES stay on the lake during these periods. Only during one day, one can see flocks of thousands of WHITE and hundreds of DALMATIAN PELICANS, thousands WHITE and hundreds of BLACK STORKS, flocks of HERONS (almost all European species), GLOSSY IBISES and SPOONBILLS, many species of DUCKS, and almost all European species of RAPTORS (hundreds of HONEY BUZZARDS and LESSER SPOTTED EAGLES, dozens of all species of HARRIERS, KITES, HAWKS, almost all species of EAGLES and FALCONS, and solitary BLACK-SHOULDERED KITES, GRIFFON VULTURES, GREAT SPOTTED EAGLES, ELEONORA'S and SAKER FALCONS). COMMON CRANES are regular on migration over the lake. The pools are very attractive to almost all species of WADERS – from abundant STINTS and SANDPIPERS (including the BROAD-BILLED, and WOOD SANDPIPER), to moderately numerous GOLDEN and GREY PLOVERS, CURLEWS, BLACK-TAILED and BAR-TAILED GODWITS, SPOTTED REDSHANKS, GREENSHANKS, MARSH SANDPIPERS, SNIPES and JACK SNIPES, RED-NECKED PHALAROPES and solitary TURNSTONES, WHIMBRELS, GREAT SNIPES. In some years, even the SLENDER-BILLED CURLEW can be seen there. Many species of GULLS can be observed too – MEDITERRANEAN, SLENDER-BILLED and LITTLE GULLS are abundant, same as all species of MARSH TERNS. Flocks of BEE-EATERS are a common picture.

Solitary ROLLERS and HOOPOES are also regular migrants. Many species of LARKS, SWALLOWS and MARTINS, PIPITS, also the THRUSH NIGHTINGALE, BLUETHROAT, ISABELLINE WHEATEAR, all species of FLYCATCHERS, LESSER GREY and WOODCHAT SHRIKES, and even AQUATIC WARBLERS can be observed.

Winter: The wintering birds of Atanasovo Lake include some RED-THROATED and BLACK-THROATED DIVERS, lots of PYGMY CORMORANTS, DALMATIAN PELICANS, BITTERN, GREAT WHITE EGRET, three species of GEESE, including the RED-BREASTED GOOSE (rarely), many species of DUCK (including some DIVING DUCKS), SANDERLING (usually on the beach of the Black Sea), BARN and SHORT-EARED OWLS, some PASSERINES.

Degree of difficulty: All described places do not require any special efforts and are very easy for observing birds by people of any degree of walking ability.

Facilities: *Fuel*: The nearest station is in the northern end of the town of Burgas (Бургас), about 1 km from the middle part of the lake.

Food: Burgas (Бургас), the nearest village Sarafovo (Сарафово) and Burgas Airport (Аерогара Бургас) provide many opportunities for different foods.

Accommodation: The nearest hotels are in Burgas (Бургас) and Sarafovo (Сарафово), where different levels of accommodation opportunities (including small private hotels) exist. Note that for the resort season (May – August) it is better to have reservation in advance.

Language: Mainly Bulgarian, but you can find English-speaking people at the Burgas Airport (Аерогара Бургас).

Status: Reserve, Ramsar Site, IBA. The banks of the nortern part of the Lake are borders of the reserve, and the area south of thee road crossing the Lake is a buffer zone, where no access is allowed too.

Permission: As a reserve, entering Atanasovo Lake at any other place than described needs a written permission from the Ministry of Environment.

Recorder: BSPB HQ.

Burgas Lake, or Vaya (Бургаско езеро или Вая)

Type: A brakish lake near the Black Sea coast, with marsh vegetation along the banks. At some places, mainly in the western part of the lake, this vegetation forms large massifs. There are some abandoned fish ponds in this area, which are specific in attracting many birds. Wet meadows exist at the northwestern end of the lake. Some agricultural fields and small patches of trees ae scattered around. In its eastern part, Vaya ends at the industrial part of the town of Burgas.

Location and strategy: The site is situated west of the town of Burgas (Бургас), near international road E87. There are many opportunities to observe birds around the lake. The best is to drive to the Burgas Free Economic Zone, and to follow an asphalt road along the bank of the lake. There are some small ponds just near the road, where interesting birds can be seen. Drive through the Free zone afterwards and take the road to Dolno Ezerovo (Долно Езерово). Right before the village there is a cart-truck, leading to the bank of the lake, where wintering WATERFOWL concentrate (be careful crossing the railway!). After the village the road crosses an area with the wet meadows. Turn to the left (to the south) at the crossroads and, after several hundred meters, stop in front of small buildings on the left-hand side from the road. This is one of the most interesting birding places - the fish farm. It is possible to enter (the people guarding the farm are familiar with birdwatchers) and make observations from the road between the pools. Another good place is an elevated point near the road just before (at its western end) the village of Gorno Ezerovo (Горно Езерово), from where there is a good panorama view over the lake.

Birds: *Breeding birds*: One of the attractions here is colony of CORMORANTS breeding on the metal pylons

Plegadis falcinellus

in the lake. It is possible to see also PYGMY CORMORANTS and WHITE PELICANS, but these two species do not breed in the lake. The BITTERN is another species which can be heard in the night, but it is easy to observe LITTLE BITTERNS flying over. The CATTLE EGRET is not breeding, but it has been seen during the last years at the fish farm. Fouraging NIGHT and SQUACCO HERONS, LITTLE and GREAT WHITE (some years) EGRETS can be seen. PURPLE HERON is breeding in the reedbeds. Such birds as the SPOONBILL, GLOSSY IBIS, RUDDY SHELLDUCK, GADWALL, GARGANEY can also be observed. Sometimes the globally endangered FERRUGI-NOUS DUCK can also be seen. Common here is the MARSH HAR-RIER. The LESSER KESTREL has been observed in the area of Gorno Ezerovo (Горно Езерово). The wet meadows are exellent for the CORNCRAKE, but in the reedbeds almost all European species of CRAKES and RALES can be seen or heard. Sometimes the BLACK-WINGED STILT and AVOCET visit the lake. The KINGFISHER is common at many places. The HOOPOE can be observed along the banks. In the villages, The SYRIAN WOODPECKER breeds. The BLACK-HEADED YELLOW WAGTAIL is common in the wet mead-ows. On the marsh vegetation and in the vegetation along the bank, good numbers of SAVI'S, CETTI'S, GREAT REED, MARSH, REED WARBLERS as well as some other WARBLERS, such as the BARRED WARBLER and OLIVACEOUS WARBLER can be identified. The PENDULINE TIT's nests are in the willows at the fish farm. CIRL and BLACK-HEADED BUNTINGS are not rare around the lake eihter.

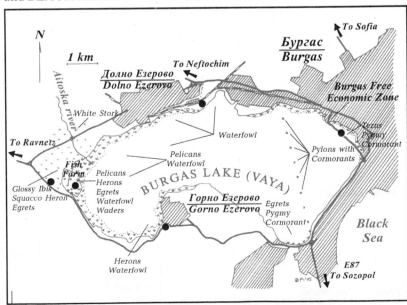

Passage: The area is very rich in birds during the passage season. It is an important stopping place for the flocks of DALMATIAN and WHITE PELIKANS, but in principle it is possible to see almost all European bird species which migrate along the western coast of the Black Sea. These include also all SOARING BIRDS, many species of DUCKS. Sometimes OSPREYS stop and fish at the fish farm, RED-FOOTED FALCONS can be seen on the wires around the lake. On some of the ponds it is possible to observe different species of WADERS, GULLS and TERNS, including BLACK, WHITE-WINGED BLACK and WHISKERED TERNS. BEE-EATERS, ROLLERS, HOOPOES, SWALLOWS and MARTINS, PIPITS, WAGTAILS, FLY-CATCHERS, different species of WARBLERS and other PASSERINES cross the area, sometimes in great numbers.

Winter: The wintering birds of Vaya include some BLACK-THROATED DIVERS, lots of different GREBES, PYGMY CORMORANTS, GREAT WHITE EGRET, some species of GEESE (including small numbers of the RED-BREASTED GOOSE), many DUCKS, especially the SHOVELER (this is a place of the highest concentration of this species in Bulgaria), but also GOLDENEYE, SMEW, other DIVING DUCKS. Sometimes the WHITE-TAILED EAGLE can be seen there. The SHORT-EARED OWL also winters in the area, as well as some PASSERINES.

Degree of difficulty: Almost all described places require no special efforts and are very easy for observing birds by people of any degree of walking ability.

Facilities: *Fuel*: The nearest station is at Burgas (Бургас), which is at about 12 km from the westernmost part of the lake.

Food: Burgas (Бургас) provides many opportunities for obtaining food. Small cafe bars, restaurants and food shops are available in the villages around.

Accomodation: The nearest hotels are in Burgas (Бургас), where there are different levels of accomodation opportunities (including small private hotels).

Language: Mainly Bulgarian.

Status: The area between the fish ponds and Gorno Ezerovo (Горно Езерово) is a reserve, the whole lake is IBA.

Permission: No access to the reedbeds of the reserve without a written permission from the Ministry of Environment. No permission is necessary to visit the described places.

Recorder: BSPB HQ.

Poda
(Пода)

Type: A coastal lagoon consisting of a mosaic of different habitats: river mouth, water pools with different levels of salinity, rich in water vegetation, patches of dry grassy land, sand beach, tree line along the road. Many other water bodies, small forests, wet meadow areas and agricultural fields exist around Poda. Some of these sites are of natural origin (Uzungeren Bay), others are quite heavily transformed (some pools were used in the recent past even for deposition of oil products from the Burgas refinery). In its northern part, Poda reaches the urban area of Burgas (Бургас).

Location and strategy: The site is situated at the very southern end of the town of Burgas (Бургас), on the Black Sea coast, in its westernmost point. For migrating SOARING BIRDS, the region of Poda is a typical 'bottle-neck' site, where (especially in autumn) migrants, following the shoreline, get concentrated in a very narrow front. The area is crossed by international road E87 to Istambul. From Burgas drive toward Sozopol (Созопол), but it is also possible to use the existing public transport. There are many opportunities to observe birds in the area. The easiest way is to stop near the road just south of a bridge and to walk to the reserve proper, following a cart-road after the old bridge. At this place, the BSPB is building a Nature Conservation and Information Centre, where you will be provided with all necessary information and material for a successful birding at the site and its surroundings. Another option is to walk some 200 m toward the sea, on the southern bank of the canal. Crossing a small forest, you will reach stony hills, which gives an excellent panorama view to the north and to the Poda Reserve itself.

Platalea leucorodia

This is the best place to observe migrating SOARING BIRDS. In winter you can continue to the bank of a nice bay, usually full of WATERFOWL. Almost the same can be said for the passage time. Interesting birds can be seen just from the area near the bridge, towards the western pools. It is possible to stop on the road between the pools, but the road is not large enough and the conditions for observing from that sector are not so good. A very good place is a small road between the pig farms and the small factory for road materials. This place can be reached from the main road from the junction south of the petrol station (take a westward direction), about 400 m after which the concrete wall of the factory ends up; stop there and walk 100 m to the bank of the Uzungeren Bay.

Birds: More than 250 species of birds have been recorded in the area around Poda. *Breeding birds* include the LITTLE GREBE, PYGMY CORMORANT (some years), LITTLE BITTERN, LITTLE EGRET, PURPLE HERON, SPOONBILL, GLOSSY IBIS (some years), POCHARD and some other DUCKS, the MARSH HARRIER, GREY PARTRIDGE, CRAKES and RALES, BLACK-WINGED STILT, AV-

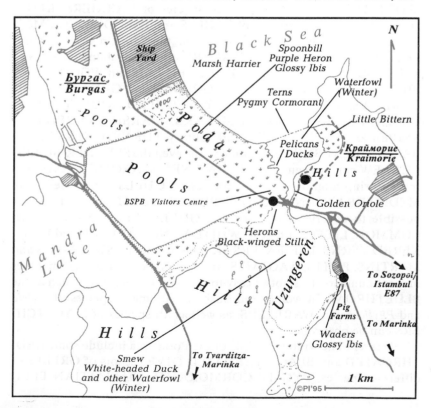

OCET, COLLARED PRATINCOLE (some years), LITTLE RINGED and KENTISH PLOVERS, COMMON and LITTLE TERNS, the KINGFISHER, TAWNY PIPIT, BLACK-HEADED YELLOW WAGTAIL (in fields around wetlands), CETTI'S, GREAT REED, MARSH, REED, OLIVACEOUS and BARRED (last two can be seen in forest and bushy areas around wetlands) WARBLERS, the BEARDED TIT, RED-BACKED SHRIKE, BLACK-HEADED BUNTING, and others. During summer time, some other, non-breeding species can be seen, like the WHITE PELICAN, SLENDER-BILLED GULL, SANDWICH and CASPIAN TERN, etc.

Passage: The area is one of the best for birding during this time. Sometimes, especially in spring, on the sea in the bay near Poda proper, it is possible to see RED-THROATED and BLACK-THROATED DIVERS. The area is used by almost all European species of GREBES. The site is also on the way of migrating WHITE and DALMATIAN PELICANS, WHITE and BLACK STORKS, almost all species of HERONS, of the GLOSSY IBIS and SPOONBILL, of many species of DUCKS (including RUDDY SHELDUCK), and almost all European species of RAPTORS (hundreds of HONEY BUZZARDS and LESSER SPOTTED EAGLES, dozens of all species of HARRIERS, KITES, HAWKS, most of the species of EAGLES and FALCONS. COMMON CRANES are regular on migration over the site. On the numerous wetlands, almost all species of WADERS stop, from abundant STINTS and SANDPIPERS (including BROAD-BILLED and WOOD SANDPIPERS) to moderately numerous GOLDEN and GREY PLOVERS, CURLEWS, BLACK-TAILED and BAR-TAILED GODWITS, SPOTTED REDSHANKS, GREENSHANKS, MARSH SANDPIPERS, SNIPES and JACK SNIPES, and solitary TURNSTONES, WHIMBRELS, GREAT SNIPES. In some years, even the SLENDER-BILLED CURLEW can be seen. Both POMARINE and ARCTIC SKUAS stop there during migration. Many species of GULLS can be seen too: MEDITERRANEAN, SLENDER-BILLED and LITTLE GULLS. It is possible to observe many TERNS: GULL-BILLED, SANDWICH, COMMON, LITTLE, BLACK, WHITE-WINGED BLACK and WHISKERED TERNS. BEE-EATERS are common there. SWALLOWS and MARTINS, PIPITS, WAGTAILS, and others cross the area, sometimes in great numbers. It is not so easy to spot some other birds, such as the BLUETHROAT. In woody and bushy areas, many species of *Sylvia* and *Phylloscopus* WARBLERS, as well as all species of FLYCATCHERS can be observed.

Winter: The wintering birds of the Poda area include some RED-THROATED and BLACK-THROATED DIVERS, lots of GREBES of different species, PYGMY CORMORANTS, DALMATIAN PELI-

CANS, the BITTERN, GREAT WHITE EGRET, all three species of
SWANS: WHOOPER, BEWICK'S and MUTE SWANS, many species
of DUCKS, including the WHITE-HEADED DUCK (the main wintering area in Bulgaria), FERRUGINOUS DUCK, GOLDENEYE,
SMEW and some other DIVING DUCKS, SANDERLING (usually
on the beach), BARN and SHORT-EARED OWLS, some PASSERINES.

Degree of difficulty: Almost all described places require no special effort and are very easy for observing birds by people of any degree of walking ability.

Facilities: *Fuel*: The nearest station is in the southern end of the
area, 200 m south of the bridge.
   Food: Burgas (Бургас) provides many opportunities for different
foods. There is a small coffee bar near the petrol station.
   Accommodation: The nearest hotels are in Burgas (Бургас), where
different levels of accommodation opportunities (including small private hotels) exist. Note that for the resort season (May - August) it is
better to have reservation in advance.
   Language: BSPB staff at the Poda Reserve speak English and Ger-
man. At the other places in the area, people speak mainly Bulgarian,
but you can find people at Burgas (Бургас) speaking English or other
foreign languages.

Status: The area between the Ship Yard, sea and the road up to
the bridge is a reserve, all described area is part of IBA.
   Permission: As a reserve managed by the BSPB, visiting Poda is
facilitated by BSPB staff there. It can provide you with very useful
information for birding in the areas outside the protected territory
too.

Recorder: BSPB HQ.

Mandra Lake
(Мандренско
езеро)

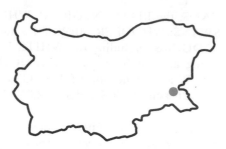

Type: A brackish-water lake of natural origin near the Black Sea coast, turned now into a reservoir with mainly fresh water. At some places there is marsh vegetation along the banks. Wet meadows exist at the western end of the lake. North of the lake, agricultural fields reach its banks, but all along the southern bank there is broad-leaved forest. In its eastern part, the Mandra Lake reaches the town of Burgas, and east of the dam of the lake there is the marshland complex of Poda – Uzungeren.

Location and strategy: The lake is situated southwest of the town of Burgas (Бургас), near the road to Sredetz (Средец). There are many opportunities to observe birds in the area of the lake. The best is to drive to the Burgas Housing Complex Meden Rudnik (комплекс Меден Рудник) and, crossing it to the south, to get to the dam of Mandra Reservoir. Some interesting birds can be seen in this area. Following the road to the village of Tvarditza (Твърдица), it is possible to stop on the hills and to take a short walk toward the lake. From Tvarditza (Твърдица) drive to the west and after 2 km from the left hand side a small marsh will be visible. This is the Reserve „Ustie na reka Izvorska" (Устие на река Изворска) which, together with the bay of the lake, is also a very good place for birding. Following an asphalt road along the bank of the lake after the village of Dimchevo, you will reach another river mouth, of the Fakiiska River (Устие на река Факийска). To get to the mouth itself, it is necessary to walk along the river some few hundred meters. Drive to the west from this place, and at the village of Debelt turn to the northeast and the road will lead

Botaurus stellaris

you to Burgas. It is possible to stop near a bridge just before the village of Novoseltzi (Новоселци), which is one of the best places to observe birds in winter.

Birds: *Breeding birds*. At several of the described places it is possible to see PYGMY CORMORANTS and WHITE PELICANS, although none of the species breeds in the lake during the last years. In the areas with reedbeds, one can observe the LITTLE BITTERN. The LITTLE EGRET can be seen too, as well as the PURPLE HERON which breeds in the reedbeds. Such birds as the SPOONBILL and GLOSSY IBIS can be observed in the area of the dam, and the RUDDY SHELDUCK on the bank of the lake from the hills north of Tvarditza (Твърдица). Within reedbeds, the MARSH HARRIER breeds. Sometimes the WHITE-TAILED EAGLE can be seen over the lake. In appropriate places and times, the wet meadows between Debelt and Novoseltzi can produce calling CORNCRAKES, and in reedbeds some other species of CRAKES and RALES can be seen or heard. The BLACK-WINGED STILT may be observed, especially near the dam or at the Izvorska mouth. An opportunity to see the KINGFISHER is the highest at the same places. A small colony of BEE-EATERS exists in the sand pits east of Novoseltzi. The HOOPOE can be observed in wooded parts of the banks. In villages, the LITTLE OWL and SYRIAN WOODPECKER breed. On marsh vegetation and on vegetation along the banks, SAVI'S, CETTI'S, GREAT REED, MARSH, REED WARBLERS and some other WARBLERS breed. In bushy areas,

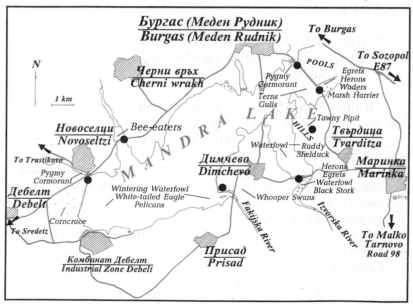

BARRED and OLIVACEOUS WARBLERS can be identified. The PENDULINE TIT can be seen at the Fakiiska River mouth. CORN, CIRL and BLACK-HEADED BUNTINGS are quite common around the lake.

Passage: The area is rich in birds during the passage season. It is an important stopping place for rest and fishing for the migrating DAL-MATIAN and WHITE PELICANS. Like at Vaya Lake, it is possible to see there almost all European species of birds migrating along the western coast of the Black Sea. This includes birds from DIVERS to PASSERINES. Quite a large number of almost all SOARING BIRDS can be seen too. The lake is very attractive to migrating DUCKS, WAD-ERS, GULLS and TERNS, including BLACK, WHITE-WINGED BLACK and WHISKERED TERNS, for BEE-EATERS, ROLLERS, HOOPOES, SWALLOWS and MARTINS, PIPITS, WAGTAILS, FLY-CATCHERS, different species of WARBLERS and other PASSERINES.

Winter: Lake Mandra supports more wintering birds in terms of both numbers and species than Lake Vaya. The species composition includes BLACK-THROATED DIVERS, almost all European species of GREBES, also the PYGMY CORMORANT, DALMATIAN PELI-CANS (in daytime they fourage on the Mandra Lake), GREAT WHITE EGRETS, all three species of SWANS, including BEWICK'S SWAN, several species of GEESE (also small numbers of the RED-BREASTED GOOSE), many DUCKS of all groups, especially the WHITE-HEADED DUCK, GOLDENEYE, SMEW. Quite regularly, the WHITE-TAILED EAGLE can be seen there. Many PASSERINES over-winter there, sometimes in flocks of thousands of birds.

Degree of difficulty: Almost all described points require no any special effort and are very easy for observing birds by people of any degree of walking ability.

Facilities: *Fuel*: The nearest stations are in Burgas (Бургас), which is at about 15 to 32 km from the westernmost parts of the lake, but they are closer to the petrol station in Sredetz (Средец), at about 11 km from the westernmost part of the lake.

Food: Burgas (Бургас) provides many opportunities for obtaining food. Small cafe bars, restaurants and food shops exist in the villages and towns around.

Accommodation: The nearest hotels are in Burgas (Бургас), where different levels of accommodation opportunities (including small pri-vate hotels) exist.

Language: Mainly Bulgarian.

Status: The area of the mouth of Izvorska River (except the road) is a reserve, the whole lake is IBA.

Permission: No access to the marsh south of the road at the Izvorska River. No permission is necessary to visit the other described places. As a fish growing lake, Mandra is under guard of a security company which preserves it from poachers, and the guards can check you. No permission is necessary for birding along the banks.

Recorder: BSPB HQ.

Chengene Skele
(Ченгене скеле)

Type: A sea bay with shallow mud flat at the mouth of a small river, covered almost completely by marsh vegetation. A small forest exists on the slopes of the low hills on both sides of the river. Some parts of the river valley are wet meadows. International road E87 crosses the site.

Location and strategy: The site is situated on the Black Sea coast about 10 km southeast of Burgas (Бургас), at the place where international road E87 almost touches the sea shore. As at the other similar places, migrants following the coastline can be observed there in quite good numbers. The best way to observe birds at this site is to stop the car near the road close to the bridge and to observe from the road. It is possible to walk to the forest or to the more open and bushy northern bank of the river, but danger of disturbing some birds exists in this case.

Birds: *Breeding birds* include the LITTLE GREBE, LITTLE BITTERN, GLOSSY IBIS (some years), CRAKES and RALES, KINGFISHER, CETTI'S, GREAT REED, MARSH, REED, OLIVACEOUS (some years) WARBLERS, RED-BACKED SHRIKE, REED BUNTING, and others. In summer some other, non-breeding species can be seen: the PYGMY CORMORANT, SQUACCO HERON, LITTLE EGRET, PURPLE HERON, SPOONBILL, MARSH HARRIER, BLACK-WINGED STIILT, SLENDER-BILLED GULL, SANDWICH, COMMON and LITTLE TERNS, etc.

Passage: Sometimes on the sea in the bay near Chengene Skele, it is possible to see RED-THROATED and BLACK-THROATED DIVERS,

Larus genei

RED-NECKED and BLACK-NECKED GREBES. Almost all species of HERONS stop in the marsh area or on the mud flat. Some species of DUCKS also use the site during this time. RAPTORS usually fly over and have no direct relation to the site itself, but some of them can be seen. This place is excellent for almost all European species of WADERS. BLACK-WINGED STIILTS, AVOCETS, RINGED, LITTLE RINGED, KENTISH, GOLDEN and GREY PLOVERS, TURN-STONE, KNOT, CURLEW SANDPIPER, DUNLIN, BROAD-BILLED SANDPIPER, LITTLE and TEMMINCK'S STINTS, RUFF, CURLEW, WHIMBREL, BLACK-TAILED and BAR-TAILED GODWITS, RED-SHANK, SPOTTED REDSHANK, GREENSHANK and WOOD SANDPIPER, COMMON, GREEN and MARSH SANDPIPERS use the mud flat for finding food during migrations. The WOODCOCK can be seen in the woody parts, and SNIPES and JACK SNIPES in the marshland area. In some years, even the SLENDER-BILLED CUR-LEW can be observed. Several species of GULLS can be seen in the bay in good numbers. From the PASSERINES, WARBLERS are regular migrants, as well as some species of FLYCATCHERS.

Winter: The wintering birds of Chengene Skele include some RED-THROATED and BLACK-THROATED DIVERS, some GREBES, GREAT WHITE EGRET, some species of SWANS, many species of DUCKS, including some DIVING DUCKS, SANDERLING, some PASSERINES.

Degree of difficulty: The described places do not require any spe-

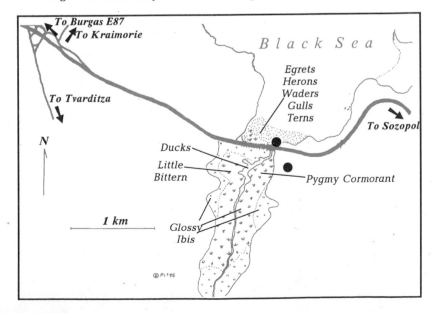

cial effort and are very easy for observing birds by people of any degree of walking ability.

Facilities: *Fuel*: The nearest station is in the southern end of Burgas (Бургас), about 10 km northward.

Food: Burgas (Бургас) provides many opportunities for different foods.

Accommodation: The nearest hotels are in Burgas (Бургас), where different levels of accommodation opportunities (including small private hotels) exist. Note that for the resort season (May - August) it is better to have reservation in advance.

Language: Mainly Bulgarian, but you can find people speaking English or other foreign languages at Burgas (Бургас).

Status: The whole area of the river including the marshland, as well as the mud flat is a reserve, IBA.

Permission: As a reserve, entering it at any place other than described needs a written permission from the Ministry of Environment.

Recorder: BSPB HQ.

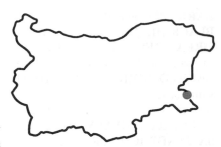

Alepu
(Алепу)

Type: A brackishwater shallow marsh with rich vegetation in a small lagoon on the Black Sea coast. Sand dunes with specific vegetation separate it from a sandy beach of the sea. From its western side the marsh is surrounded by wet meadows and agricultural fields, and by the holiday village of Dyuni in its northern part.

Location and strategy: The lake is situated near the holiday village of Dyuni, which is about 8 km south of the town of Sozopol (Созопол), on international road E87 (Konstantsa – Istambul). The site is good for observing migrating SOARING BIRDS along the Black Sea coast. In autumn they appear at relatively low heights over the hills north of the marsh. It is easy to find there some good point (free access) and to observe migrants coming from the north from close distance. Another good point are the dunes in the northern part of the marsh (near a small bridge), where it is possible to observe birds inhabiting dunes, marsh as well as migrating and sea birds at the same time. It is possible also to observe migrants even from a proper balcony of the hotel in Duni or from the terrace of a cafe bar up there. An asphalt road surrounds the marsh from the west and provides good opportunities for observing birds, especially in the second half of the day.

Anthus campestris

Birds: _Breeding birds_ include RED-NECKED and LITTLE GREBES, PYGMY CORMORANT (some years), LITTLE BITTERN, PURPLE HERON, MARSH HARRIER, CRAKES AND RALES, LITTLE RING PLOVER (on the beach), SCOPS OWL and NIGHTJAR (both in the forested area west of the marsh), KINGFISHER, BEE-EATER (northward, close to Sozopol), ROLLER (rarely), HOOPOE, WRYNECK, GREY-HEADED, GREEN, MIDDLE SPOTTED, SYRIAN and LESSER SPOTTED WOODPECKERS, WOOD-

LARK (all in woodland and „garden" areas), TAWNY PIPIT (in dunes), BLACK-HEADED YELLOW WAGTAIL (in agricultural fields), CETTI'S, GREAT REED, MARSH, REED, OLIVACEOUS (in vegetation along the banks and in the holiday village) and BARRED WARBLERS, RED-BACKED SHRIKE, BLACK-HEADED BUNTING, and others. During summer time some other, non-breeding species can be observed, such as the LITTLE EGRET, SPOONBILL, GLOSSY IBIS. In some years, YELKOUAN SHEARWATERS can be seen over the sea, where non-breeding SANDWICH TERNS can also be observed. Soaring LESSER SPOTTED EAGLE can be seen over the hills west of the marsh.

Passage: Like other parts of the Black Sea coast, the area is excellent for birding during the whole spring and autumn. Almost all European species of GREBES use the lake and the sea in this period. It is possible to observe large numbers of WHITE and DALMATIAN PELICANS, WHITE and BLACK STORKS, almost all European species of HERONS, flocks of GLOSSY IBIS and SPOONBILLS, many species of DUCKS, and almost all European species of RAPTORS. Flocks of COMMON CRANES migrate over the beach. The area attracts many species of WADERS, such as the BLACK-WINGED STIILT, AVOCET, KENTISH PLOVER, RUFF, REDSHANK, SPOTTED REDSHANK, GREENSHANK, WOOD SANDPIPER, MARSH SANDPIPER, WOODCOCK, SNIPE and JACK SNIPE. Some GULLS can be seen in the area, including MEDITERRA-

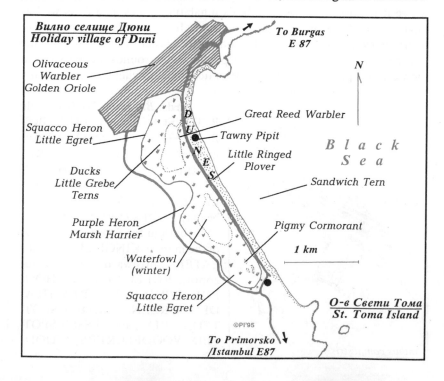

NEAN, SLENDER-BILLED, and LITTLE GULLS, as well as almost all species of TERNS: SANDWICH, COMMON and LITTLE TERNS, but this is a very good place to observe from close distance and in big flocks BLACK, WHITE-WINGED BLACK and WHISKERED TERNS. Flocks of BEE-EATERS are common on passage, as well as solitary ROLLERS and HOOPOES. SWALLOWS and MARTINS migrate on numerous passages. The wet areas around are good for PIPITS and WAGTAILS, while the bushy parts are used by WHINCHAT, STONECHAT, many species of WARBLERS and SHRIKES, on tree vegetation all species of FLYCATCHERS can be observed.

Winter: The wintering birds of the area are very interesting too. On the sea, it is possible to see RED-THROATED and BLACK-THROATED DIVERS, BLACK-NECKED GREBE, many RED-BREASTED MERGANSERS. The marsh is preferred by PYGMY CORMORANTS, sometimes by BITTERN, GREAT WHITE EGRET, some species of DUCKS (including GADWALL and some DIVING DUCKS). Chances for observing WHITE-TAILED EAGLE are quite high there. The beach is a wintering site for the SANDERLING. Some PASSERINES also winter in the area.

Degree of difficulty: All described places do not require any special efforts and are very easy for observing birds by people of any degree of walking ability.

Facilities: *Fuel*: The nearest station is in Sozopol (Созопол), about 8 km from the site.

Food: During the resort season (April – September) the holiday village of Dyuni (Дюни) offers many possibilities, but they are limited over the rest of the year. Many opportunities exist in the town of Sozopol (Созопол).

Accommodation: Many hotels of different classes are available both in the holiday village of Dyuni (Дюни) and in the town of Sozopol (Созопол). There are also several camping sites around. Note that for the peak of the season (May – August) it is better to have reservation in advance.

Language: Mainly Bulgarian, but you can find people speaking English or other foreign languages at the holiday village of Dyuni (Дюни), in Sozopol (Созопол) and in the camping sites along the coast.

Status: Reserve, IBA. The banks of the Lake are the borders of a reserve.

Permission: No access to the marsh itself, but there is free access to all described places around.

Recorder: BSPB HQ.

Ropotamo
(Ропотамо)

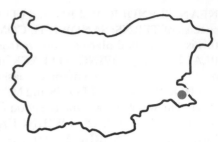

Type: A mosaic of different habitats on the Black Sea coast. Flooded forests of old beech, oak and other trees, with abundant lianas and bushes on the banks of Ropotamo River, and several small marshes together with a broad-leaved forest on the hills around form the main habitat. A sandy beach ends in its southern part with high sand dunes. Ropotamo River has several meanders with rich marsh vegetation before joining the sea. Some small marshes and rivers exist within the forest, several rocky areas can be seen on the slopes.

Location and strategy: Ropotamo is situated about 50 km south of Burgas (Бургас) and 20 km of Sozopol (Созопол), on international road E87. There are two main places where all interesting birds can be seen. First is the parking area in the northern part of the reserve. At some 100 m there is small path into the forest, leading to the platform in the marsh of Arkutino (Аркутино), where one of the observation points is located. The second opportunity is to follow the road to the south from this place, and just after the bridge over Ropotamo River to turn to the left toward the parking area within the forest. Nearby you will see a small quay for boats, where in summer it is possible to get a small boat to the mouth of the river.

Haliaetus albicilla

Birds: *Breeding birds*: The BITTERN and LITTLE BITTERN, GREAT WHITE EGRET (in some years), PURPLE HERON, MARSH HARRIER, LITTLE and SPOTTED CRAKES, CETTI'S, GREAT REED, MARSH and REED WARBLERS can be seen in marsh areas, the BLACK STORK, WHITE-TAILED and LESSER SPOTTED EAGLE, HOBBY, GREY-HEADED, GREEN,

MIDDLE SPOTTED, GREAT SPOTTED and LESSER SPOTTED
WOODPECKERS, SOMBRE TIT, SHORT-TOED TREECREEPER and
TREECREEPER in woodlands, LITTLE RINGED PLOVER breeds
on the beach, the SCOPS and EAGLE OWL can be heard in the night,
as well as the NIGHTJAR. Along the river, the KINGFISHER is common. On sand dunes, the SHORT-TOED LARK and TAWNY PIPIT
can be seen. Ropotamo is one of the places where such species as the
SEMI-COLLARED FLYCATCHER and OLIVE-TREE WARBLER
breed.

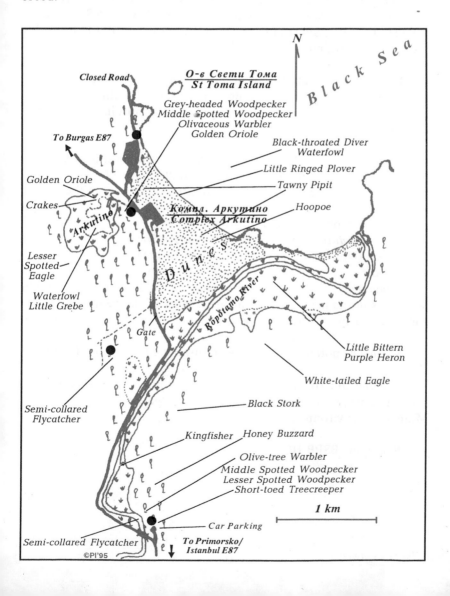

Passage: Ropotamo is similar to all other sites along the Bulgarian Black Sea coast, where it is possible to see an enormous variety of migrating species: from the GREBES, YELKOUAN SHEARWATER, CORMORANTS at the sea, all soaring species, including PELICANS, STORKS and RAPTORS, non-soaring birds as HERONS, EGRETS, GLOSSY IBIS and SPOONBILL, various WATERFOWL, CRANES, many WADERS, GULLS and TERNS, large numbers of PASSERINES.

Winter: On the sea or on the river and marshes, quite a lot of birds can be seen: DIVERS, GREBES, CORMORANTS, GREAT WHITE EGRET, some WATERFOWL, some RAPTORS including WHITE-TAILED, SPOTTED and even LESSER SPOTTED EAGLES (as an exception), etc.

Degree of difficulty: Both described ways for birding in the area are very easy for people with all degrees of walking abilities. There are many possibilities for short walks around, but the most interesting birds can be seen just from the road.

Facilities: *Fuel*: The nearest possibility to obtain it is in Sozopol (Созопол), which is at a distance of about 20 km.

Food: There are many opportunities to obtain food in the resorts around, but close to the birding places proper there are almost no possibilities to obtain food and drinks.

Accommodation: The nearest hotels are in Sozopol (Созопол) and Primorsko (Приморско), but it is better to have reservation in advance if the visit is to be during the resort season.

Language: Almost no people speaking English or other foreign languages in the main part of the area. Most of the people in the resorts around speak foreign languages.

Status: Ropotamo is a reserve, Ramsar Site (Arkutino Marsh) and IBA.

Permission: To enter the reserve at any place other than the described above, it is necessary to have a written permission from the Ministry of Environment.

Recorder: BSPB HQ.

Studen Kladenetz (Студен кладенец)

Type: A deep and rocky valley of Arda River in the low mountain area of the Eastern Rhodopi, surrounded by open stony slopes and hills, at some places covered by bushes and small low broad-leaved forests, with screes, small dry valleys and cliffs, rocks and rocky massifs. There are a few small villages around.

Location and strategy: The Studen Kladenetz (Студен кладенец) Dam is situated about 40 km south of Haskovo (Хасково) or about 50 km westsouthwest of the Svilengrad (Свиленград) cross-border between Bulgaria, Greece and Turkey. The best way to reach the site is to turn south from E80 near Haskovo (Хасково) and to drive via Knizhovnik (Книжовник), Stambolovo (Стамболово), Goliam Izvor (Голям Извор), Madzhari (Маджари), where about 2 km after the village a sharp turn to the right must be followed for Studen Kladenetz (Студен кладенец). When the dam of the Studen Kladenetz Reservoir becomes visible, you can stop at one of the best viewing places on the left side of the road. Another good place is at the dam itself. One of the VULTURE upfeeding places, established by the Bulgarian Society for the Protection of Birds, is situated in the area, and to visit it, it is necessary to drive to the village of Potochnitza (Поточница), to turn left in front of the school building in the centre, to drive straight on, and at the end of the village, to follow the cart-track (not very flat!) to the place, where a concrete platform will show you a „Vulture restaurant". It is better for this visit to get in touch with the BSPB in advance in order the visit to be more successful.

Ciconia nigra

Birds: More than 160 bird species have been recorded in the site. From a point of view of *breeding birds*, this is one of the very few Bulgarian sites with the presence of three species of Vultures: GRIFFON (about 50 individuals), EGYPTIAN (5-7 individuals) and BLACK VULTURES (1-6 individuals), usually over the hills south of the dam. This is one of the richest areas for BIRDS OF PREY: individual IMPERIAL, GOLDEN, SHORT-TOED, BOOTED and LESSER-SPOTTED EAGLES, PEREGRINE can be seen, some individuals of LONG-LEGGED and HONEY BUZZARD, GOSHAWK, SPARROWHAWK, HOBBY, LESSER and COMMON KESTREL can also be observed flying or soaring over the valley. The site is attractive to BLACK KITES, single OSPREYS and, given good chance, even the WHITE-TAILED SEA EAGLE can be seen. The site is significant also with a breeding density of the BLACK STORK which is one of the highest in Europe (more than 7 nests on the cliffs around) and with a rock nesting colony (3-5 pairs) of the GREY HERON. The group of birds of southern origin is quite well represented too: the CHUKAR, PALLID SWIFT (breeding under the roof of the Post Office in the village near the dam), SYRIAN WOODPECKER (common in all villages), BLUE ROCK THRUSH (along the bank near the eastern edge of the dam), SOMBRE TIT (in the forest north of the dam), ROCK NUTHATCH (in a rocky valley below the dam), SUBALPINE, SARDINIAN and

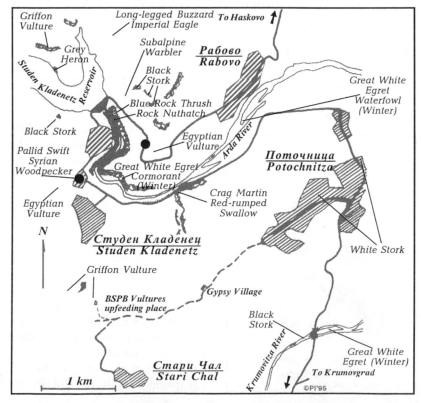

OLIVACEOUS WARBLERS (in bushes on slopes east and northeast of the dam), BLACK-HEADED BUNTING (often on wires along the road), etc. SCOPS OWLS can be heard during the night, some LITTLE OWLS even during the day often stay on chimneys in all villages. The KINGFISHER, BEE-EATERS, HOOPOES can be seen. The region supports one of the most clean (most close to the wild type) ROCK DOVES in Bulgaria.

Passage: HERONS and EGRETS, some RAPTORS, including HOBBY, RED-FOOTED FALCONS, HARRIERS, BLACK KITES, and others, fly along the Arda Valley. The WOODCOCK, SNIPE, GARGANEY and some other WATERFOWL migrate over it. SEMI-COLLARED and PIED FLYCATCHERS, some LEAF WARBLERS are quite common on passage.

Winter: High numbers of GREAT WHITE EGRETS (up to 70 birds altogether) can be seen on the banks and on the rocks below the Power Station, often together with CORMORANTS. The BLACK-THROATED DIVER (rarely), LITTLE GREBE and some WATER-FOWL overwinter some years on the waters of the reservoir. In late winter, calling EAGLE OWLS can be heard west of the dam.

Degree of difficulty: There are many possibilities for short walks around the place along the paths, but the most interesting birds can be seen just from the road.

Facilities: *Fuel*: Haskovo and Krumovgrad are the nearest possibilities to obtain it.

Food: It is better to get supplied in advance with food and drinks for a stay at the site.

Accommodation: At the moment the nearest hotel is in Krumovgrad (Крумовград), which is at about 25 km.

Language: Almost no people speaking English or other foreign languages. Most of the people speak a local dialect of Turkish.

Status: The whole area is IBA, the territory of the hills east, west and south of the village of Studen Kladenetz and north and west of the feeding platform near Potochnitza is a reserve.

Permission: No access to the reserve without a written permission of the Ministry of Environment. The other described places are open to the public.

Recorder: BSPB HQ.

Arda River bridge near Kotlari (Моста на Арда при Котлари)

Type: An open valley of the Arda River (река Арда) between the dam of Studen Kladenetz Reservoir (язовир Студен кладенец) and the village of Kotlari (Котлари), surrounded by limestone rocks and forested hills, with a metal construction bridge. Several water bodies on the northern bank of Arda have been created by excavation of sand and shingle at the sand pits there. The area is situated in the low mountain part of the Eastern Rhodopi. Nearby is the mouth of Krumovitza River (река Крумовица). Several small villages are located around.

Location and strategy: The Arda River bridge near Kotlari (Котлари) is situated about 45 km south of Haskovo (Хасково) on a way to Studen Kladenetz (Студен кладенец) (about 5 km south of the crossroads from Madzhari (Маджари) to Studen Kladenetz) or to Krumovgrad (Крумовград) via Padalo (Падало). The best way to reach the site is to turn to the South from E80 near Haskovo (Хасково) and to drive via Knizhovnik (Книжовник), Stambolovo (Стамболово), Goliam Izvor (Голям Извор), Madzhari (Маджари), to continue straight ahead at the crossroads to Krumovgrad (Крумовград) and Studen Kladenetz (Студен кладенец) (it is about 2 km after Madzhari). You can stop near the road in front of a picturesque rock with many artificial niches on the left-hand side. Another good observation point is near the sand pits on the northern bank of the river, about 200 m east of this site, the entrance is just in front of the buildings near the road to Dolno Cherkovishte (Долно Черковище). Some birds can also be seen just from the road on the southern bank of Arda, but there are only a few safe places to stop there.

Apus melba

Birds: *Breeding birds.* The short distance between this site and the Studen Kladenetz Dam makes the lists of the birds very similar. Here it is also possible to see three species of Vultures flying together: GRIFFON, EGYPTIAN and BLACK VULTURES (rarely). as well as solitary IMPERIAL, SHORT-TOED, BOOTED and LESSER-SPOTTED EAGLES. The GOSHAWK, SPARROWHAWK, HOBBY, LESSER and COMMON KESTREL can also be observed over the valley. The BLACK STORK is a common bird in the area and it can be seen fishing in the river near the bridge. The WHITE STORK breeds in Dolno Cherkovishte (Долно Черковище), where also the SYRIAN WOODPECKER can be seen. The LITTLE RINGED PLOVER is a common breeder on the Arda River bed. In forested parts on the slopes and along the river, the NIGHTJAR and SOMBRE TIT are possible to be seen, and within some of the patches of mediterranean vegetation, SUB-

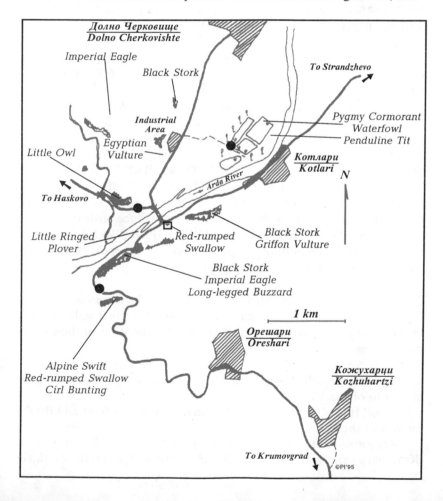

ALPINE, SARDINIAN and OLIVACEOUS WARBLERS occur. Besides chimneys in the villages, the LITTLE OWL can be seen in the niches of the rock near the bridge. On the rocks on the southern bank of Arda River, the ALPINE SWIFT, CRAG MARTIN, RED-RUMPED SWALLOW and some other rocky birds breed. SCOPS OWLS can be heard during the night. Near the river there are sites where the KINGFISHER can be seen. On slopes, the WOOD LARK can be observed, and the SKYLARK over fields with crops. The HOOPOE is also not a rare bird on the river banks. Some interesting birds can be observed at the sand pits' pools. These are the PENDULINE TIT, GREAT REED WARBLER, REED BUNTING. CORN, CIRL and BLACK-HEADED BUNTINGS are abundant in the area, also the ORTOLAN and ROCK BUNTINGS can be observed.

Passage: Almost all species of HERONS and EGRETS, some RAPTORS, including HOBBY, RED-FOOTED FALCONS, HARRIERS, BLACK KITES, and others fly over the river or use vegetation on the banks for roosting. The COMMON and GREEN SANDPIPER, WOODCOCK, SNIPE as well as the WIGEON, GARGANEY, SHOVELER, POCHARD, TUFTED DUCK, GOOSANDER and some other WATERFOWL use the river valley and the ponds during migration. SEMI-COLLARED and PIED FLYCATCHERS, some LEAF WARBLERS are quite common on passage.

Winter: Fishing GREAT WHITE EGRETS can be seen on the river, CORMORANTS and PYGMY CORMORANTS in the sand pit. The same habitat is occupied by LITTLE, GREAT CRESTED, RED-NECKED and BLACK-NECKED GREBES, and some WATERFOWL overwinter some years on the waters of the pit. Once birds of all three swan species, MUTE, BEWICK'S and WHOOPER SWANS, have been seen together in the pool of the pit. On the nearest rocks, GRIFFON VULTURES roost during some windy and cold days.

Degree of difficulty: Most of the described birds can be seen just from the road, but there are many possibilities for short walks around the river on paths. Easy for almost all people regardless of their walking abilities.

Facilities: *Fuel*: Haskovo and Krumovgrad are the nearest possibilities to obtain it.

Food: It is better to get supplied in advance with food and drinks for stay at the site.

Accommodation: The nearest hotel is in Krumovgrad (Крумовград), which is at about 37-45 km dependent on the road, via

Padalo (Падало) or via Studen Kladenetz (Студен кладенец), respectively.

Language: Almost no people speaking English or other foreign languages. Most of the people speak a local dialect of Turkish.

Status: Reserve, IBA. The slopes along the southern bank of Arda River and the cliffs on both sides of the river are under protection.

Permission: Not required for the places described above. The area around the bridge is open to the public. To enter the pits with a car, it is necessary to ask the man from the building in front of their entrance near the road to open the barrier (no problem about this).

Recorder: BSPB HQ.

Madzharovo (Маджарово)

Type: A deep and rocky valley of Arda River in the low mountain area of the Eastern Rhodopi. A relatively narrow, stony and sandy river bed of Arda River is surrounded by hills, covered by low broad-leaved forests and bushes, with screes, small dry valleys and cliffs, rocks and rocky massifs. There are mines in the area, a small town and a few small villages.

Location and strategy: Madzharovo (Маджарово) is a small miner's town situated about 65 km south of Haskovo (Хасково) or about 52 km westsouthwest of the Svilengrad (Свиленград) cross-border between Bulgaria and Greece and Turkey. The best way to reach the site is to turn south from E80 near Haskovo (Хасково) and to drive via Knizhovnik (Книжовник), Stambolovo (Стамболово), Goliam Izvor (Голям Извор), Silen (Силен) where, before the end of the village, there is a well-signed turn to the left. Follow the road and turn to the right near the beginning of Dolni Glavanak (Долни Главанак), cross the village, and the road will lead you to the Arda River valley near Madzharovo (Маджарово). Cross the bridge and, after a small monument, turn to the left (do not drive to the town itself) and after some 100 m turn again to the left on a cart-truck through the forest. Some 300 m further you will reach one of the best viewing places: the slopes of a tiny hill over a the sharp turn of the river and in front of the biggest rocky massif in the area. This is also one of the VULTURE feeding places, established by the Bulgarian Society for the Protection of Birds, and it will be better to contact the BSPB HQ in advance, if you want to coordinate your visit with the upfeeding of the VULTURES. Another good opportunity is to drive along the

Gyps fulvus

road to Borislavtzi (Бориславци) and to stop at suitable places near the road itself. From the very southern end of the village of Borislavtzi (Бориславци) the shallow part of the Ivailovgrad Reservoir (язовир Ивайловград) with some interesting birds can be observed. Near the bridge, the BSPB is building a nature conservation and information centre, where you will be provided with all necessary information and materials for a successful birding in that area.

Birds: *Breeding birds.* The site is one of the places with the highest breeding density of the BLACK STORK in Bulgaria. The WHITE STORK breeds in Borislavtzi (Бориславци). The site is very rich in RAPTORS: it is possible to see BLACK KITES, EGYPTIAN, BLACK and GRIFFON VULTURES (up to 50 individuals over the valley), some LONG-LEGGED BUZZARDS, GOLDEN, SHORT-TOED and BOOTED EAGLES, the HOBBY, LESSER KESTREL and PEREGRINE can also be seen. During the last years, even the OSPREY has been observed there. The CHUKAR is often calling from the rocks. BLACK-WINGED STILT can be seen sometimes on the bank of Ivailovgrad Reservoir (язовир Ивайловград) near Borislavtzi (Бориславци). The LITTLE RINGED PLOVER is a common breeder on the river bed. The ROCK DOVE, LITTLE OWL, NIGHTJAR, ALPINE SWIFT, KINGFISHER, HOOPOE, WRYNECK, MIDDLE SPOTTED and SYRIAN WOODPECKERS can easily be seen in the relevant habitats. SCOPS OWLS can be heard during the night everywhere in the area. Along the rock faces, the CRAG MARTIN and RED-RUMPED SWALLOWS fly in good numbers. The STONECHAT, BLACK-EARED WHEATEAR, ROCK and BLUE ROCK THRUSHES, SUBALPINE, BARRED, SARDINIAN and ORPHEAN WARBLERS, SOMBRE TIT, ROCK NUTHATCH, RED-BACKED,

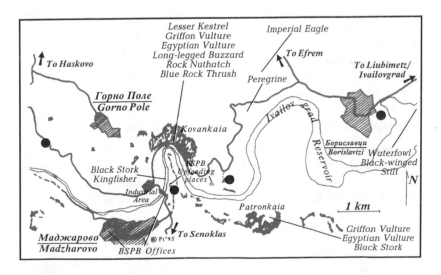

LESSER GREY and WOODCHAT SHRIKES, GOLDEN ORIOLE, numerous HAWFINCHES, CIRL, ROCK and BLACK-HEADED BUNTINGS complete the picture.

Passage: LITTLE and GREAT CRESTED GREBES, the PYGMY CORMORANT, almost all species of HERONS and EGRETS, some DUCKS, many RAPTORS, including BLACK KITES, EGYPTIAN and GRIFFON VULTURES (in 1993 also the LAMMERGEIER), all species of HARRIERS, the HONEY BUZZARD, WHITE-TAILED EAGLE, LESSER SPOTTED, BOOTED, SHORT-TOED EAGLES, the OSPREY, HOBBY, RED-FOOTED FALCONS, and others fly along the Arda River valley. Several species of WADERS can be seen on the banks of the reservoir, and the WOODCOCK in the forested areas on the slopes. BEE-EATERS and many species of PASSERINES follow the valley on their migratory route. Among the most interesting are SEMI-COLLARED and PIED FLYCATCHERS, some LEAF WARBLERS, some FINCHES, etc.

Winter: Regular on wintering are GREAT WHITE EGRETS, in some years on the Ivailovgrad Reservoir (язовир Ивайловград) WHOOPER SWANS and some other WATERFOWL overwinter. The WHITE-TAILED EAGLE during this season. GRIFFON and, sometimes, BLACK VULTURES remain in the area too, as well as the ROCK NUTHATCH, RAVEN, and others.

Degree of difficulty: There are many possibilities for short walks around the place along paths, but the most interesting birds can be seen just from the road.

Facilities: *Fuel*: The nearest petrol station is in the town of Madzharovo (Маджарово).

Food: It is better to get supplied in advance with food and drinks for a stay at the site. Some opportunities exist in Madzharovo (Маджарово), but they are limited.

Accommodation: There is no hotel at Madzharovo (Маджарово), so the best is to plan Haskovo (Хасково) (65 km) or Svilengrad (Свиленград) (52 km) as places to overnight.

Language: Almost no people speaking English or other foreign languages. Most of the people speak a local dialect of Turkish.

Status: The main rocky complexes are reserves, the area is IBA.

Permission: Not required for the places recommended as observation points. No access close to the big rocks and rocky complexes. Many places are dangerous due to abandoned mine galleries.

Recorder: BSPB HQ.

Dolna Kula
(Долна Кула)

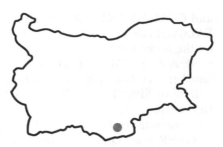

Type: The upper part of the valley of Krumovitza River (река Крумовица) between Krumovgrad (Крумовград) and the mouth of the river, surrounded by volcanic cliffs on steep hills, open terrains and lands covered with dry grass and scrub on the western bank of the river, and by agricultural lands on the open valley of Krumovitza on its eastern side, ending with open, dry and scrubby hills. The area includes a sandy and shingle bed of Krumovitza, covered at some places with *Tamarix* bushes and a tree and bush vegetation along the banks. Several small villages are located around.

Location and strategy: The site is situated near the village of Dolna Kula (Долна Кула), which is about 15 km north of Krumovgrad (Крумовград). From Krumovgrad take the road to Kardzhali (Кърджали), about 4 km after that you will cross a bridge over Krumovitza River. From the centre of the village, just after this bridge, called Gorna Kula (Горна Кула), turn to the right and follow an asphalt road along the river. Coming from Haskovo (Хасково) – Kardzhali (Кърджали), turn to the left at Gorna Kula (Горна Кула) before reaching Krumovgrad (Крумовград). You can stop near the road at any place after the village up to the end of the asphalt (some 10 km). The rock faces after the second village are the most interesting site for observation.

Coracias garrulus

Birds: *Breeding birds.* The short distance between this site and the Studen Kladenetz Dam makes its raptor list quite similar. This is another place where it is possible to see three species of Vultures flying together: GRIFFON, EGYPTIAN and BLACK VULTURES (rarely). Sometimes the SHORT-TOED EAGLE, LONG-LEGGED BUZZARD, GOSHAWK, SPARROWHAWK, HOBBY, LESSER and COMMON KESTRELS, PEREGRINE and even ELEONORA'S FALCON can be observed over the hills. The BLACK STORK breeds on the rocks and it can be seen quite close fishing in the river near the road. A nest of WHITE STORK exists on a concrete pilon in the village between Gorna Kula and Dolna Kula just near the road. A small colony of SPANISH SPARROWS breeds within its nesting material. In the river bed, in the area of the small cemetery before Dolna Kula, sometimes the STONE-CURLEW can be seen. The LITTLE RINGED PLOVER is a common breeder in the bed of Krumovitza River. In the area, quite clean (close to the real wild birds) ROCK DOVES exist. The place is one of the very few in Bulgaria where GREAT SPOTTED CUCKOOS have been observed, even „breeding". The WRYNECK, GREEN, LESSER SPOTTED WOODPECKERS represent their group along the river. In the scrubby areas on the slopes, the STONECHAT, OLIVE-TREE, OLIVACEOUS, SUBALPINE, BARRED, SARDINIAN, ORPHEAN WARBLERS, LESSER WHITETHROAT and WHITETHROAT, SOMBRE TIT, RED-BACKED, LESSER GREY, WOODCHAT and MASKED (very rarely) SHRIKES can be seen together.

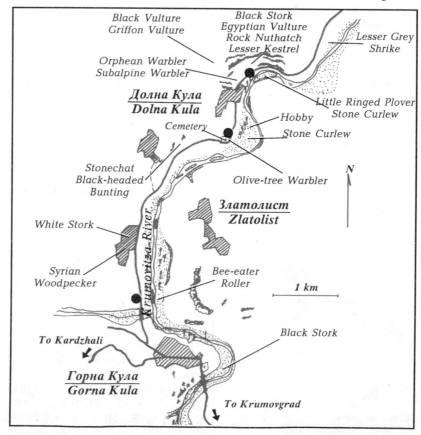

On the rocks near Dolna Kula, the CRAG MARTIN, RED-RUMPED SWALLOW, ROCK NUTHATCH breed. On the river banks, the KINGFISHER can be seen, and in the trees along Krumovitza, ROLLER and HOOPOE breed. CORN, CIRL and BLACK-HEADED BUNTINGS are abundant in the area, sometimes also the ORTOLAN can be observed there.

Passage: Almost all species of HERONS and EGRETS, some RAPTORS, including HARRIERS, BLACK KITE, HOBBY, RED-FOOTED FALCONS, and others follow the valley during migrations, and some (especially HERONS and EGRETS) roost on vegetation along the river. Sometimes the COMMON and GREEN SANDPIPERS and the WOODCOCK can also be seen. Flocks of BEE-EATERS regularly fly along the valley on both spring and autumn migrations. Many PASSERINES, including COLLARED, SEMI-COLLARED and PIED FLYCATCHERS, STONECHAT, WHINCHAT, some LEAF WARBLERS, are quite common on passage.

Winter: In some winters GREAT CRESTED GREBES can be seen on the river. Fishing GREAT WHITE EGRETS are regular in the area, some GREEN SANDPIPERS remain for wintering there. The area lies in a region regularly searched by GRIFFON and BLACK VULTURES for food.

Degree of difficulty: Most of the described birds can be seen just from the road, but there are many possibilities for short walks along the river. Easy for almost all people regardless of their walking abilities.

Facilities: *Fuel*: At the moment Krumovgrad (Крумовград) is the nearest possibility to obtain it.

Food: It is better to get supplied in advance with food and drinks for a stay at the site.

Accommodation: At the moment the nearest hotel is in Krumovgrad (Крумовград), which is at about 15 km.

Language: Almost no people speaking English or other foreign languages. Most of the people speak a local dialect of Turkish.

Status: IBA.

Permission: Not required. The area along the river is open to the public. It is not recommended to claim the hills towards the rock face near Dolna Kula, nor to walk on the river bed in order to avoid disturbance of some birds there.

Recorder: BSPB HQ.

Rogach
(Рогач)

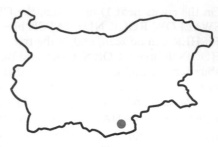

Type: Open, dry, rocky mountain hills north of the road from Krumovgrad (Крумовград) to Ivailovgrad (Ивайловград) in the region of the village of Rogach (Рогач). Rocky walls of volcanic type on the slope just near the village are the most interesting areas. The slopes are covered by dry-type grasses and scrubs. Some tobacco plantations and other agricultural lands surround the road.

Location and strategy: The site is situated about 8 km east of Krumovgrad (Крумовград). Following the direction to Ivailovgrad (Ивайловград), the road reaches one relatively long and straight part. Almost at the end of it, at something as a tiny valley it is necessary to turn left and to enter a short asphalt sector (about 50 m) on the road junction to the village Rogach Kaialakioi (Рогач Каялъкьой). Leave the car there and follow the road to the village, cross it and reach the last yard with a big tree there, at the foot of the slope. This is a good place to observe, but you can also walk some 100 m (not more, danger of disturbing birds!) on the slope towards the rock wall.

Birds: *Breeding birds.* The area is inhabited by the EGYPTIAN VULTURE, CHUKAR, QUAIL (in crops), ROCK DOVE, LITTLE OWL (in the village), SCOPS OWL, HOOPOE, WRYNECK (in gardens around), GREEN and SYRIAN WOODPECKERS. Small patches of oak trees are good for the WOODLARK. On the rocky face, the CRAG MARTIN, RED-RUMPED SWALLOW, ROCK NUTHATCH and BLACK REDSTART breed (in the town of Krumovgrad (Крумовград), which is the starting point, there are REDSTARTS of the race *samamisicus* breeding). In scrubby areas on the slopes, the STONECHAT, OLIVACEOUS, SUBALPINE, BARRED, SARDINIAN, ORPHEAN WARBLERS, LESSER WHITETHROAT and WHITETHROAT,

Monticola saxatilis

SOMBRE TIT, RED-BACKED and WOODCHAT SHRIKES can be seen. In spite of the NORTHERN WHEATEAR, black-throated and white throated forms of BLACK-EARED WHEATEAR can be observed on the slopes. On the rock wall, ROCK THRUSH, BLUE ROCK THRUSH and RAVEN breed. CORN, CIRL and BLACK-HEADED BUNTINGS are abundant in the area.

Passage: A few species only, mainly on spring migration. The site is not on a migratory route. More regular are flocks of BEE-EATERS, some PASSERINES, including COLLARED, SEMI-COLLARED and PIED FLYCATCHERS, some LEAF WARBLERS, etc.

Winter: A few birds remain, but the ROCK NUTHATCH, sometimes BLUE ROCK THRUSH, rarely GRIFFON VULTURES do.

Degree of difficulty: Most of the described birds can be seen relatively easily, but a 700-m long walk on a slightly slopy and not asphalted surface makes observations difficult for some people.

Facilities: *Fuel*: Krumovgrad (Крумовград) is the nearest possibility to obtain it.

Food: It is better to get supplied in advance with food and drinks for a stay at the site.

Accommodation: The nearest hotel is in Krumovgrad (Крумовград), which is at about 8 km from the place.

Language: Almost no people speaking English or other foreign languages. Most of the people speak a local dialect of Turkish.

Status: No special statute.

Permission: Not required. The area is open to the public. It is not recommended to claim the hills closely to the rock wall in order to avoid disturbance of some birds there.

Recorder: BSPB HQ.

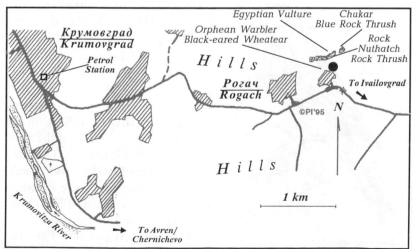

Visokata Pesht
(Високата пещ)

Type: A former limekiln (turned into a restaurant) on the bank of Chaya River (река Чая), in a place where the valley of a small river coming from the east joins a deep limestone valley of Chaya. The site is surrounded by quite various habitats. To the north there are relatively open and dry rocky hills with low trees and bushes, to the south steep slopes are covered by mixed forest, to the west there are very steep slopes with ruins of a Medieval fortress and churches. Rich vegetation on banks of the rivers. The road from Plovdiv (Пловдив) to Smolyan (Смолян) follows the Chaya River bank.

Location and strategy: The site is situated at about 3 km south of Asenovgrad (Асеновград). The limekiln is very easy to be identified by its high chimney. Turn to the building and leave the car in a car park in front of the restaurant. Almost all birds can be seen just from this place, but a short walk upstream a smaller valley can be fruitful for some other species.

Birds: *Breeding birds.* From the car park it is possible to see

Emberiza cia

different birds, dependent on the time you can spend there. It is possible to observe the SPARROWHAWK and GOS-HAWK (rarely), HONEY and LONG-LEGGED BUZZARDS. Sometimes the SHORT-TOED EAGLE and PEREGRINE can be seen over the hills north of the place. The HAZEL GROUSE exists in the higher parts of the area, but it is difficult to see it. The same concerns the EAGLE OWL which, at the beginning of the breeding season, can be heard calling closer to the town of Asenovgrad (Асеновград) proper. The AL-

PINE SWIFT is common around cliffs with the ruins west of the car park. In relevant times, a singing WOODLARK can be heard. Over the valley, the CRAG MARTIN and RED-RUMPED SWALLOW can be seen, along the river the GREY WAGTAIL and DIPPER occur. The BLACK REDSTART often sings from the rocks bellow the ruins. The area is excellent for observing the BLUE ROCK THRUSH, which breeds in the stone-pit behind the building of the limekiln (in some years, the ROCK THRUSH can be seen too). The SOMBRE TIT also inhabits the area. It is possible to see CIRL and ROCK BUNTINGS at this place in bushy areas with scarce trees at the entrance of a smaller valley.

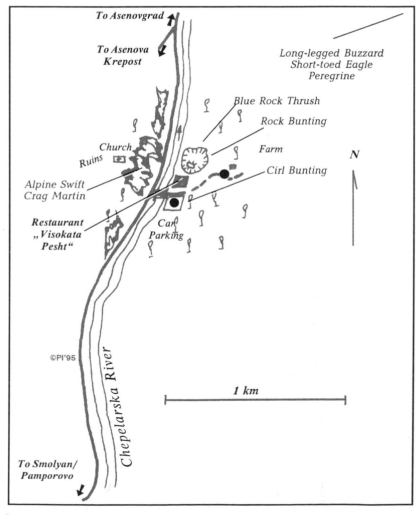

Passage: Quite a good number of species, mainly PASSERINES, migrate through the area. The valley of Chaya, which is oriented from north to south, has some importance as a second-class migratory route. Most often species include SWALLOWS and MARTINS, PIPITS, almost all species of WAGTAILS, WHEATEARS, WARBLERS, COLLARED, SEMI-COLLARED and PIED FLYCATCHERS, some SHRIKES, FINCHES, etc.

Winter: Few birds remain, but the ROCK BUNTING, sometimes the BLUE ROCK THRUSH, DIPPER, and others can be seen.

Degree of difficulty: Most of the described birds can be seen very easily, just from the car park, by people of any degree of walking abilities.

Facilities: *Fuel*: The nearest petrol station is at the southern end of Asenovgrad (Асеновград), at about 2 km.

Food: If the restaurant is closed or not appropriate, Asenovgrad (Асеновград) suggests many opportunities for different foods and drinks.

Accommodation: The nearest hotels are in Asenovgrad (Асеновград), which is at 2 km.

Language: Almost no people speaking English or other foreign languages. At the restaurant or in Asenovgrad (Асеновград), you can find some people speaking foreign languages.

Status: No special statute.

Permission: Not required. The area is open to the public.

Recorder: BSPB HQ.

Topolovo
(Тополово)

Type: Open slopes of the Rhodopi Mountains and dry pastures near the village of Topolovo (Тополово), covered with low grasses, bushes and small groups of trees. The site is close to a small reservoir and some other small wetlands, from its northern side it is surrounded by agricultural lands, and from its southern side by forested hills.

Location and strategy: The site is situated near a road at the northwestern end of the village of Topolovo, about 17 km from Asenovgrad (Асеновград) on the road to Kardzhali (Кърджали). You can stop near the road before a small bridge in the beginning of the village and to walk several hundred meters southward on the slope along a cartroad or through the pastures.

Birds: *Breeding birds.* The main bird to be seen there is the ISABELLINE WHEATEAR, a small colony of which breeds in holes of Susliks. There it is also possible to see a flying IMPERIAL EAGLE. The WHITE STORK breeds in the villages around, where also the SYRIAN WOODPECKER and LITTLE OWL can be observed. The LITTLE RINGED PLOVER is the only wader in the area. In the forested part on the slopes, it is possible to see the NIGHTJAR, SOMBRE TIT, on the slopes also the WOODLARK, while the SKYLARK over fields with crops. SCOPS OWLS can be heard in the area during the night. The HOOPOE and sometimes the ROLLER breed in trees. The TAWNY PIPIT, BARRED WARBLER, WOODCHAT SHRIKE, GOLDEN ORIOLE,

Lanius senator

RAVEN, HAWFINCH, CORN, CIRL and BLACK-HEADED BUN-TINGS are common in the area.

Passage: Some species of SOARING BIRDS migrate over the area, mainly RAPTORS, including HONEY BUZZARDS, HOBBY, HARRIERS, and others. The COMMON SANDPIPER can be seen on banks of reservoirs, and WOODCOCK in forested parts. Many PASSERINES, including SEMI-COLLARED and PIED FLYCATCHERS, some LEAF WARBLERS are quite common on passage.

Winter: Fishing GREAT WHITE EGRETS can be seen sometimes on banks of reservoirs. The GREAT GREY SHRIKE can be observed in winter there too.

Degree of difficulty: Most of the described birds can be seen after a very easy walk or from the road.

Facilities: *Fuel*: The nearest opportunity is in the village of Topolovo (1 km from the site).

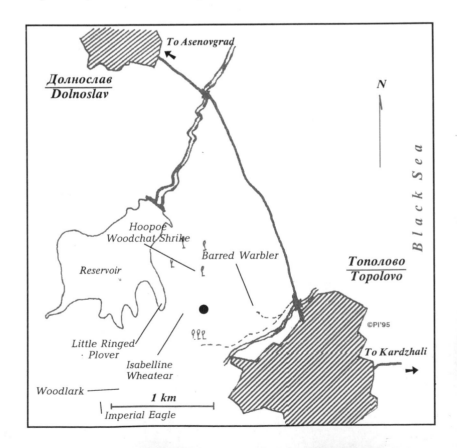

Food: There are some small bars in Topolovo and many opportunities in Asenovgrad, but it is better to get supplied in advance with food and drinks for a stay at the site.

Accommodation: The nearest hotels are in Asenovgrad (Асеновград), which is at about 17 km distance.

Language: Almost no people speaking English or other foreign languages. Most of the people speak a local dialect of Turkish.

Status: No special statute.

Permission: Not required. The area is open to the public.

Recorder: BSPB HQ.

Dobrostan Hills (Добростански рид)

Type: Mountain hills with a mosaic of habitats: an open calcareous plateau and slopes, cliffs and rock faces, a deep valley, mountain meadows, broad-leaved, mixed and coniferous forests, small mountain villages.

Location and strategy: Dobrostan Hills (Добростански рид) is a quite large area situated south of the town of Asenovgrad (Асеновград). To reach its best birding part, it is necessary to take the road to Kardzhali (Кърджали) and, at the end of the village of Cherven (Червен), on a well-signed crossroads, to take to the right (to the south) towards Dobrostan (Добростан)/Mostovo (Мостово). At the end of the village of Oreshetz (Орешец) take to the right to the village of Dobrostan (Добростан) and follow the mountain road (not all asphalted, but possible for cars) to the village. Just before it you can stop for the ROCK THRUSH and some other birds. Afterwards cross the village and, by an asphalt road, you will reach the mountain hut Martziganitza (хижа Марциганица). From the hut it is possible to have walks following the paths, but the best is to follow the path downstairs to an open area (about 100 m from the hut), afterwards take the cart-road to the left (to the southwest) and follow it keeping the highest part of the hill. At about 800 m you will reach a cliff over the valley, from the top of which cliff you can see most of the local highlights.

Pyrrhocorax graculus

Birds: *Breeding birds*: The GOSHAWK, LONG-LEGGED BUZZARD, GOLDEN and IMPERIAL (in the lower parts) EAGLES, HOBBY, LESSER KESTREL, PER-

EGRINE can be seen over the valley. The HAZEL GROUSE and ROCK PARTRIDGE occur in the region, but to see them, more time and special preparations are required. The STOCK DOVE, SCOPS and LITTLE OWLS, NIGHTJAR, ALPINE SWIFT, HOOPOE, WRYNECK (in the village of Dobrostan), WOODLARK, CRAG MARTIN, TREE PIPIT, BLACK-EARED WHEATEAR, ROCK THRUSH and BLUE ROCK THRUSH, CRESTED TIT, ALPINE CHOUGH, RAVEN, SERIN, SISKIN, ROCK BUNTING and some other species make the place quite exotic for Western Europeans.

Passage: Mainly PASSERINES, but also BEE-EATERS, some RAPTORS.

Winter: The most interesting birds are the CRESTED TIT, ALPINE CHOUGH, some RAPTORS.

Degree of difficulty: Medium, as there is some walk up to the cliff at the edge of the valley. Many of the birds can be seen from the road.

Facilities: *Fuel*: The nearest possibilities to obtain it are in Topolovo (Тополово), 25 km, but more sure is Asenovgrad (Асеновград), 32 km.

Food: It is better to get supplied in advance with foods and drinks for the whole stay at the site.

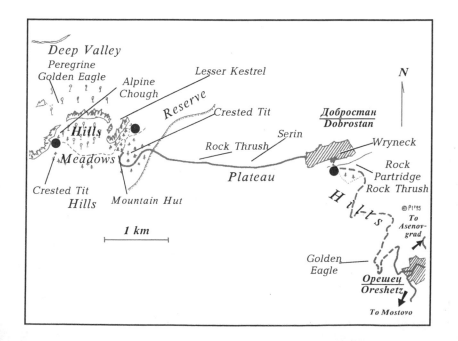

Accomodation: The nearest hotels are in Asenovgrad, which is at about 32 km, some modest conditions to overnight exist during the warmer part of the year in the Martziganitza mountain hut.

Language: Almost no people speaking English or other foreign languages.

Status: The area around the mountain hut is part of a nature reserve.

Permission: To visit the reserve, it is necessary to have a written permission from the Ministry of Environment. The area around the road before the mountain hut is open to the public.

Recorder: BSPB HQ.

Pamporovo
(Пампорово)

Type: A high-montane area
(1 500-2 000 m a.s.l.) of the
Western Rhodopi (Западни Родопи) Mountains. The site includes
coniferous forests, mixed with some grassy slopes and mountain
meadows. Hotels and other buildings of the winter resort
Pamporovo (Пампорово), connected with asphalt roads, are scattered in the forest. There are several small streams in the area.

Location and strategy: The ski resort Pamporovo (Пампорово)
is situated at about 14 km north of Smolyan (Смолян) and at about 90
km south of Plovdiv (Пловдив). From both sites, there are good road
signs both in Cyrillic and Latin scripts. It is possible to come to the
area also by international road E79 via Gotze Delchev (Гоце Делчев)
— Dospat (Доспат) — Devin (Девин) — Shiroka laka (Широка лъка).
To observe birds in the area of the resort, it is necessary to simply
walk along roads, but it is possible also to enter the forest at some
places on cart-trucks or forester paths. To reach the top Snezhanka
(Снежанка) surmounted by a retranslation tower, it is possible to walk
along an asphalt road,
along the path below the
lifts or to use chair lifts.
From the tower, one can
walk westward, cross a
meadow and an asphalt
road (possible to use if
you prefer to walk down
to the resort itself), go
slightly upward through
the forest and, following
the same direction, you
can reach Orpheus' Rocks
(Орфееви скали) with a
beautiful panorama view
to the Smolyan Lakes
(Смолянски езера) and
to the Mursalitza Hills
(рида Мурсалица).

Loxia curvirostra

Birds: *Breeding birds*: BLACK STORKS sometimes fly over the resort, SPARROWHAWKS and GOSHAWKS can rarely be seen at any place of the area. The STOCK DOVE can be seen regularly. Several species of OWLS exist in the area, but most often it is possible to see the TAWNY OWL and the SCOPS OWL (the latter can be observed even on some of the hotels as Perelik, for example). NIGHTJAR is another bird which can be observed easily. Sometimes several birds can be seen catching insects around the lamps near the main street in front of the Murgavetz Hotel. The site is very good to observe the PALLID SWIFT, dozens of which breed under the roof of hotels (Prespa Hotel for example) and can be watched from very short distance in good light. Similar is the situation with the BLACK WOOD-

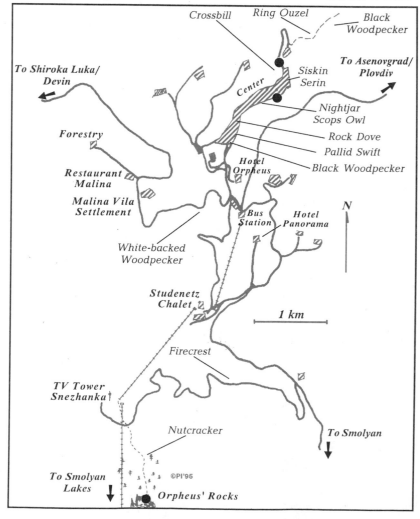

PECKER which can also be seen in trees just near the road or in front of the balcony. With a better chance, the WHITE-BACKED WOOD-PECKER of the subspecies *lilfordi* can be seen too. Many interesting PASSERINES can be observed from short distance at relevant habitats: WOODLARK, CRAG MARTIN, RED-RUMPED SWALLOW, GREY WAGTAIL, DIPPER (both along streams), BLACK REDSTART (abundant), RING OUZEL (in coniferous forest in the higher northern part of the resort), SONG and MISTLE THRUSHES, GOLDCREST and FIRECREST, MARSH, WILLOW and CRESTED TITS, TREECREEPER, RED-BACKED SHRIKE, NUTCRACKER (in the forest area on the top of Snezhanka), RAVEN, SERIN, SISKIN, BULLFINCH, LINNET, CROSSBILL, YELLOWHAMMER, and others.

Passage: The area is situated on a migratory route of various birds. BLACK and WHITE STORKS and even GREY HERONS fly over the site. Around the tower at Snezhanka, ELEONORA'S FALCON has been observed, but speaking about regular birds, they are mainly PASSERINES (but also BEE-EATERS). Most regular are SWALLOWS and MARTINS, PIPITS, THRUSHES, ICTERINE, WOOD and WILLOW WARBLERS, several species of FLYCATCHERS, some SHRIKES and FINCHES.

Winter: There are not too many birds, but from close distance and without special efforts it is possible to see several species of WOODPECKERS, the RING OUZEL, GOLDCREST, FIRECREST, CRESTED TIT, NUTCRACKER (closer to buildings during this period), CROSSBILLS, and others.

Degree of difficulty: There are many possibilities for shorter or longer walks around the place along roads or paths, some very easy, others quite difficult and requiring special preparations, but the most interesting birds can be seen just from the road.

Facilities: *Fuel*: There is a petrol station in the resort itself, but make sure about its working hours.

Food: There is good choice for obtaining different foods — from different sorts of restaurants to a small food shop in the resort.

Accommodation: There are many different level hotels in the area.

Language: Mainly Bulgarian, but it is possible to find many people speaking English or other foreign languages, especially at hotels.

Status: No special statute.
Permission: Not required.

Recorder: BSPB HQ.

Trigrad Gorge (Триградско ждрело)

Type: A deep and narrow mountain gorge with vertical calcareous cliffs (up to 200 m high), with slopes covered with scarce or dense coniferous forests, with a fast stream.

Location and strategy: The Trigrad Gorge (Триградско ждрело) is situated in the Western Rhodopi Mountains near the border with Greece, about 64 km west of the town of Smolyan (Смолян) and at 12 km from the crossroads near the village of Teshel (Тешел). From the resort Pamporovo (Пампорово) drive toward Shiroka Laka (Широка лъка) — Devin (Девин), before Devin (Девин) turn to the left (to the west), cross a small bridge before Devin's quarter Nastan (Настан) and follow the road to the crossroads near another small bridge and road signs Teshel (Тешел) (no village there, but small buildings on both sides of the road). Drive straight on (do not turn to the right to Borino (Борино)) and you will reach an extremely narrow part, where the road enters a tunnel in a cliff. Stop about 100 m after the tunnel at a small parking area near the entrance of a cave called Devil Throat (Дяволското гърло), and you will be at the place. From Plovdiv (Пловдив) drive toward Krichim (Кричим), follow the road to Devin (Девин), when approaching it, do not enter the town itself, but drive straight on to the crossroads near the bridge before its quarter Nastan (Настан). Later follow the road as described above. The best place for observing birds is the parking area and the higher part of the road just before the village of Trigrad (Триград). Most of the birds can be observed there without a walk around. Another option is to go to the village of Trigrad (Триград), to cross the river and to walk eastward along a stony road (note that in this case you will enter a border area).

Tichodroma muraia

Birds: *Breeding birds*: Both SPARROWHAWK and GOSHAWK can be seen, sometimes the GOLDEN EAGLE (look for it along the road after Devin), SHORT-TOED EAGLE, HOBBY, LESSER KESTREL (can be seen around Nastan), PEREGRINE, STOCK DOVE (rarely), ALPINE SWIFT (around the cliff near Nastan and in the Trigrad Gorge itself), KINGFISHER (at some areas of the river with still water), BLACK WOODPECKER, WOODLARK, CRAG MARTIN (abundant everywhere, nests on the cliff near Nastan), RED-RUMPED SWALLOW (abundant), GREY WAGTAIL (abundant along streams and the river), DIPPER (quite common along streams), BLACK REDSTART (common). The site is the best for observing the WALLCREEPER from short distance. One option is from the car parking, sometimes birds appear just near the entrance of the cave or fly over the valley and can be observed moving on the cliff faces. The WALLCREEPER can be seen also at the wall of the southern end of the tunnel near the parking area. Probably the best place is several km north of it, where there is a spring on the eastern side of the road,

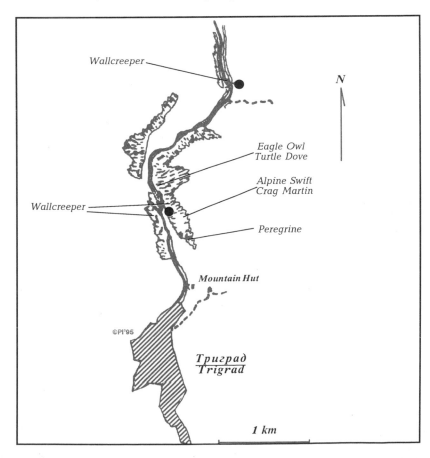

together with a local fork on the road. Leave the car there and walk 150 m northward along the main road to a place where this road has a bridge, joining the two cliffs of the gorge. Often the WALLCREEPER can be seen there from 10 – 15 m distance. From other birds, more interesting are the RED-BACKED SHRIKE, RAVEN, CIRL and ROCK BUNTINGS, etc.

Passage: Many of the above birds can be seen during the period of migration, they are resident. Some other birds can be seen only during this time: the GREY HERON or BLACK STORK, some RAPTORS, BEE-EATERS, ICTERINE, GARDEN, WOOD, WILLOW WARBLERS, CHIFFCHAFF, PIED, COLLARED, SEMI-COLLARED and SPOTTED FLYCATCHERS, GOLDEN ORIOLE, NUTCRACKER (dozens of them can be seen flying southward in September), FINCHES, etc.

Winter: The bird composition is not very rich, but some of the main birds of the area can be seen, including the WALLCREEPER, especially in more mild winters.

Degree of difficulty: There are some possibilities for short walks around the place as described above, but the most interesting birds can be seen just from the road. Suitable for people of any walking abilities.

Facilities: *Fuel*: The nearest possibilities to obtain it is in Devin (Девин), which is at about 27 km.

Food: It is better to get supplied in advance with food and drinks for a stay at the site. There are good opportunities for obtaining different foods in Devin (Девин), including some small restaurants. A small coffee bar exists near the entrance of the cave.

Accommodation: The nearest hotels (including small private ones) are in Devin (Девин), which is at about 27 km. Many opportunities in this respect exist in the winter resort Pamporovo (Пампорово), at about 50 km from the site, but during the tourist season it is better to have reservation in advance.

Language: Almost no people speaking English or other foreign languages.

Status: The site around the cave is a reserve.

Permission: Not required. Approaching the cliffs at any place other than described is not allowed without a written permission of the Ministry of Environment. No access to the inner parts of the border area.

Recorder: BSPB HQ.

Rusenski Lom near Ivanovo (Русенски Лом при Иваново)

Type: A deep canyon with limestone cliffs and meanders of the Rusenski Lom River (река Русенски Лом) in the region of the village of Ivanovo (Иваново). The canyon is about 200 m wide on the average and is situated in a plain area with huge agricultural lands, and in fact it is completely under their level. The river itself is 3-5 m wide, surrounded by quite rich vegetation on the banks, large fields and meadows. The valley can be entered and left at specific places only. The mixture of habitats also includes some small ponds with marsh vegetation, some bushy areas and several villages around.

Location and strategy: The village of Ivanovo (Иваново) is situated about 20 km south of the town of Ruse, 4 km off the road Ruse - Sofia (road E85). From the northern end of Ivanovo, at a well signed crossroads to Skalna Tzurkva (Скална църква), it is necessary to drive eastward to the lowest part of the valley. Leave the car at a small parking place and follow a stony staircase to the platform on the cliff with an ancient church in the cave. Following the path you will reach an exellent viewing place on the cliff. Another option is to walk along the river into the valley itself.

Birds: *Breeding birds.* In some years, the RUDDY SHELLDUCK breeds in the holes of the rock cliff just near the main viewing point. The LEVANT SPARROWHAWK, HONEY BUZZARD, LONG-LEGGED BUZZARD, SHORT-TOED EAGLES, HOBBY and even SAKER can be seen in flight around. The PHEASANT is very common in the valley. The STOCK DOVE

Tadorna ferruginea

is also possible to be seen. In a relevant period of the year and of the journey, one can hear EAGLE and SCOPS OWLS in the valley, while the LITTLE OWL can be seen in the villages around. The ALPINE SWIFT can be spotted flying in the sky, the KINGFISHER, BEE-EATER, ROLLER, HOOPOE, WRYNECK, GREY-HEADED, MIDDLE SPOTTED, LESSER SPOTTED and SYRIAN WOOD-PECKER are other possible birds. From among the most interesting PASSERINES, the WOODLARK, CRAG MARTIN, RED-RUMPED SWALLOW, TAWNY PIPIT, BLACK-EARED WHEATEAR, BARRED WARBLER, SOMBRE TIT, several species of FINCHES, BLACK-HEADED BUNTING, etc., are to be mentioned.

Passage: The valley of Rusenski Lom River is situated on a secondary migration route of birds, and many migrants can be seen there. Even several species of HERONS and EGRETS, flocks of BLACK and WHITE STORKS, almost all species of RAPTORS follow the valley and warm air flows rising from the surrounding lands. Some other NON-PASSERINES and especially abundant PASSERINES use vegetation in the valley during the migration period.

Winter: Wintering GREEN SANDPIPERS can be seen along the river, sometimes the resident LONG-LEGGED BUZZARD, KING-FISHER and some other birds, mainly PASSERINES.

Degree of difficulty: Almost all described birds can be seen just from the described viewing places or from the road, which makes the site easy for almost all people regardless of their walking abilities.

Facilities: *Fuel*: The town of Dve Mogili (Две могили), about 18

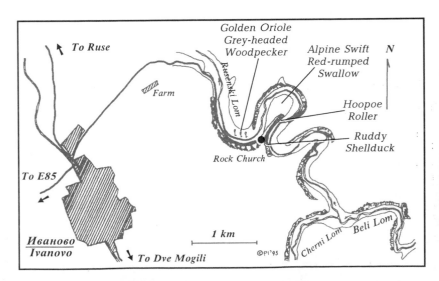

km from the site, and Ruse (Pyce), about 20 km are the nearest places to obtain it.

Food: There are many opportunities to get food in the area, mainly in the above towns, but it would be no bad idea to supply yourself in advance with food and drinks for a stay at the site.

Accommodation: The nearest hotels are in Dve Mogili (Две могили) and in Ruse (Pyce), where it is possible to find different levels of accommodation.

Language: Almost no people speaking English or other foreign languages. Only along the E85 road some people speak foreign languages.

Status: The site is a part of the National Park Rusenski Lom.

Permission: Despite the fact that it is part of a national park, no permission is needed to get to the described site.

Recorder: BSPB HQ.

Kalimok
(Калимок)

Type: Fish ponds in the place of a large marsh in the past, some remains of which have been preserved. Situated on the Danube River bank, separated from the river by a belt of almost natural riparian vegetation. Wet meadows exist west and south of the ponds. Some agricultural fields of the nearest village surround the site from the southern side.

Location and strategy: The site is situated near the road from Ruse (Русе) to Silistra (Силистра), close to the village of Nova Cherna (Нова Черна), which is about 12 km west of the town of Tutrakan (Тутракан). There are two main opportunities to observe birds there. The best is to turn to the north on an asphalt road before entering the village of Nova Cherna (Нова Черна) if you are coming from Tutrakan (Тутракан), to follow the road, and after some 800 m you will reach a small bridge over a drainage canal. Leave the car just after it and walk along the concrete belts between the pools (best along the belt leading to the west, along the canal). It is possible also to walk from the bridge straight northward and to reach Danube River. The second way is to enter the village of Nova Cherna (Нова Черна) and to cross it to the north, to follow a cart-road leading to the canal and to reach an area of wet meadows.

Egretta alba

Birds: *Breeding birds*. It is possible to see from very short distance all species of GREBES, including RED-NECKED and BLACK-NECKED (on nests) GREBES, the PYGMY CORMORANT, DALMATIAN PELICAN (often visiting the area), to hear the BITTERN or to

observe LITTLE BITTERNS often flying over vegetation, sometimes
fouraging NIGHT and SQUACCO HERONS, LITTLE and GREAT
WHITE (some years) EGRETS, PURPLE HERONS. Such birds as the
SPOONBILL, GLOSSY IBIS, GREYLAG GOOSE, RUDDY SHEL-
DUCK, GADWALL, GARGANEY can also be observed in good numbers. A common bird there is the FERRUGINOUS DUCK as well as
the MARSH HARRIER. Visitors from the Danube islands and banks
come sometimes to the ponds: the BLACK KITE, WHITE-TAILED
EAGLES. If you have enough time and patience, it is possible to hear
or even see some CRAKES and RALES. Breeding here are the BLACK
(some years) and the WHISKERED (big colony) TERNS. The KING-
FISHER is common along the drainage canal, but the ROLLER and
HOOPOE can also be observed there. In the village, SYRIAN WOOD-
PECKER breeds, along the Danube it is easy to find GREY-HEADED
and MIDDLE SPOTTED WOODPECKERS. On marsh vegetation and
on vegetation along the canal, a good number of GREAT REED,
MARSH, REED WARBLERS, some SAVI'S and GRASSHOPPER
WARBLERS as well as the BARRED WARBLER can be identified.
The PENDULINE TIT's nests are in the willows along the canal.

   Passage: The area is also very good for observing migrating birds
along the Danube River. During the breeding season, it is possible to
see almost all European species of GREBES, also WHITE and BLACK
STORKS, almost all species of HERONS, many species of DUCKS,
and almost all European species of RAPTORS: dozens of HONEY
BUZZARDS and LESSER SPOTTED EAGLES, all species of HAR-
RIERS, BLACK KITES, all species of HAWKS, some migrating
BOOTED and SHORT-TOED EAGLES, the OSPREY and several spe-

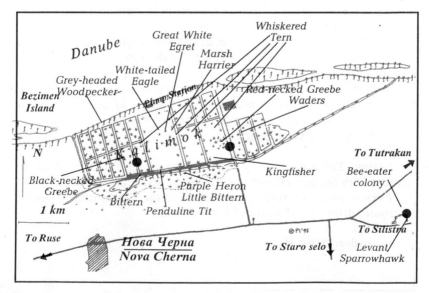

cies of FALCONS: RED-FOOTED FALCON, HOBBY, SAKER (rarely), and others. On the shallow ponds it is possible to observe large numbers of different species of WADERS - BLACK-WINGED STILTS, LITTLE RINGED, GOLDEN and GREY PLOVERS, CURLEW, WOOD and MARSH SANDPIPERS, WHIMBREL, GODWITS, SPOTTED REDSHANKS, GREENSHANKS. There as well as in vegetation along the banks of the pools, SNIPES and JACK SNIPES can be seen. Some GULLS (including the LITTLE GULL) as well as many European species of TERNS can be observed during this period, including BLACK, WHITE-WINGED BLACK and WHISKERED TERNS. BEE-EATERS, ROLLERS, HOOPOES, SWALLOWS and MARTINS, PIPITS, WAGTAILS, FLYCATCHERS, different species of WARBLERS and other PASSERINES cross the area sometimes in great numbers.

Winter: The wintering birds of Kalimok include some BLACK-THROATED DIVERS, lots of different GREBES, PYGMY CORMORANTS, the GREAT WHITE EGRET, some species of GEESE (sometimes quite large numbers of WHITE-FRONTED and GREYLAG GEESE), many DUCKS, especially the GOLDENEYE, SMEW, GOOSANDER, other DIVING DUCKS. The WHITE-TAILED EAGLE is a regular wintering bird there. The SHORT-EARED OWL sometimes can be seen, as well as some PASSERINES.

Degree of difficulty: Almost all described places do not require any special effort and are very easy for observing birds by people of any degree of walking ability.

Facilities: *Fuel*: The nearest station is in Tutrakan (Тутракан), which is at a distance of about 12 km.

Food: Tutrakan (Тутракан) provides some opportunities for obtaining food. A small cafe bar and a food shop exist in the village of Nova Cherna (Нова Черна).

Accommodation: The nearest hotels are in Tutrakan (Тутракан) and Silistra (Силистра), where different levels of accommodation opportunities (including small private hotels) exist.

Language: Mainly Bulgarian.

Status: The area of the ponds, the canal and the wet meadows together with the nearest island on Danube River are a reserve, IBA.

Permission: As a reserve, no access to the site without a written permission from the Ministry of Environment.

Recorder: BSPB HQ.

Malak Preslavetz (Малък Преславец)

Type: A small reservoir on the Danube River bank, covered by various types of marsh vegetation, including water lilies and other floating plants. The slopes of the valley are covered by broad-leaved forest, some wet meadow areas exist near a shallow part at the southern end of the reservoir. Some loess walls are near the road between the reservoir and the nearest village with the same name.

Location and strategy: The site is situated on the Danube bank itself, north of the village of Malak Preslavetz (Малък Преславец). The village is near the road from Ruse (Русе) to Silistra (Силистра), at about 34 km northeast of Tutrakan (Тутракан). To reach the site, turn northward near the petrol station at the eastern end of the village of Zafirovo (Зафирово), follow an asphalt road to Malak Preslavetz (Малък Преславец), where, in the centre, turn to the left (to the west) and follow an asphalt road to the Danube. Leave a car near the buildings in front of the pump station and walk along the cart-road along the bank of the reservoir (turning to the west, along the Danube bank). At the end of the dam (about 300 m from the car), turn to the south and, following a cart-road, enter the forest on the bank of the reservoir to watch some woodland birds.

Birds: *Breeding birds.* It is possible to see quite a good variety of birds in spite of the fact that some of them do not breed in the reservoir itself, but use it as a feeding site. Among the most interesting birds are the RED-NECKED and BLACK-NECKED GREBES, the PYGMY CORMORANT, DALMATIAN PELICAN (fishing on the Danube

Chlidonias hybrida

bank some 500 m west of the dam), LITTLE BITTERN, fouraging NIGHT and SQUACCO HERONS and LITTLE EGRETS, PURPLE HERONS, the MARSH HARRIER, BLACK KITE. There is a big colony of several dozen to a few hundred pairs of WHISKERED TERNS. Other breeding species are the KINGFISHER, BEE-EATER (in the loess near the road), HOOPOE (along the Danube), GREY-HEADED, MIDDLE SPOTTED and LESSER SPOTTED WOOD-PECKERS. In the areas with marsh vegetation, GREAT REED and REED WARBLERS breed, and in the forest on the western bank of the reservoir, the SOMBRE TIT can be seen.

Passage: The area is very good for observing migrating birds along the Danube River. Migrating PYGMY CORMORANTS fly over the river sometimes in quite large numbers, WHITE and BLACK STORKS, HERONS follow their route over the site. Many DUCKS can be observed both on river and reservoir. The area is crossed by many Euro-

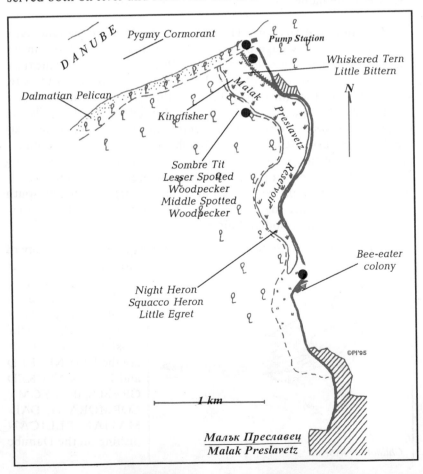

pean species of RAPTORS, including HONEY BUZZARDS and LESSER SPOTTED EAGLES, HARRIERS, BLACK KITES, HAWKS, the OSPREY, several species of FALCONS. Some GULLS and TERNS fly across the area in large numbers. Quite typical here are the waves of BEE-EATERS, SWALLOWS and MARTINS, FLYCATCHERS, WARBLERS and other PASSERINES.

Winter: The wintering bird fauna of Malak Preslavetz proper depends on the weather and, when the reservoir freezes, it is quite poor. But on the Danube, usually there are concentrations of large numbers of different species of DUCKS, especially when the level of the river is not very high and there are sand bars. Sometimes GEESE (mainly WHITE-FRONTED and GREYLAG GEESE) also come for roosting on the Danube in this area. These concentrations attract WHITE-TAILED EAGLES, and sometimes the SPOTTED EAGLE winters too.

Degree of difficulty: The described places do not require any special effort and are very easy for observing birds by people of any degree of walking ability.

Facilities: *Fuel*: The nearest station is at Zafirovo (Зафирово), which is at about 14 km.

Food: Tutrakan (Тутракан) and Silistra (Силистра) provide various opportunities for obtaining food.

Accommodation: The nearest hotels are in Tutrakan (Тутракан) and Silistra (Силистра), where different levels of accommodation opportunities (including small private hotels) exist.

Language: Mainly Bulgarian.

Status: The area of the reservoir is a reserve, IBA. The banks of the reservoir are borders of a protected territory.

Permission: As a reserve, no access to any place other than described is allowed without a written permission from the Ministry of Environment.

Recorder: BSPB HQ.

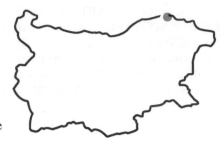

Srebarna
(Сребърна)

Type: A large marsh on the right bank of Danube River, separated from the river by a belt of partly natural riparian vegetation, and by small agricultural fields and wet areas. On the hills surrounding the marsh there are small forests, mainly of *Robinia pseudoacacia*, mixed with grassy areas. The small island Komluka is also part of the reserve. The southern part of the marsh reaches the village of Srebarna (Сребърна).

Location and strategy: The site is situated near the road from Ruse (Русе) to Silistra (Силистра), at about 18 km west of the latter town. There are several opportunities to observe birds in the area. The easiest way is to stop near the road just south of the marsh (there is a small parking place near a spring there) and to observe the birds in this part of the wetland. During some years, the biggest colonies of PYGMY CORMORANTS, HERONS, IBISES, SPOONBILLS are just near the bank of the marsh, and the view from that place is excellent. The place is good as an initial one because it gives a very good panorama of the whole marsh and the opportunity to plan the birding in the area according to the particular situation with the birds seen on the wetland. A second possibility is to go to the village, following the signs to reach the buildings of the Administration of the reserve and the small museum (unfortunately, with stuffed birds and other animals), to leave the car at the parking there, to go downstairs near the

Pelecanus crispus

building of the museum and follow the cart-road on the western bank of the marsh (about 2 km toward the Danube River). To watch the DALMATIAN PELICAN colony, it is necessary to go up the slope when it is possible to reach the middle part of the western bank of the marsh, and crossing the small forest you will reach a higher open place, from which PELICANS can be seen on the nests. This is also one of the best places to observe migrating SOARING BIRDS during the relevant seasons. Another option is to stop and leave the car near the place where the road from Silistra (Силистра) crosses the southeasternmost corner of the marsh and to follow the cart-road along the eastern bank of Srebarna.

Birds: More than 180 species of birds have been recorded in Srebarna and its nearest surroundings. *Breeding birds* include RED-NECKED and BLACK-NECKED (some years) GREBES, the PYGMY CORMORANT, DALMATIAN PELICAN, BITTERN, LITTLE BITTERN, NIGHT and SQUACCO HERONS, LITTLE and GREAT

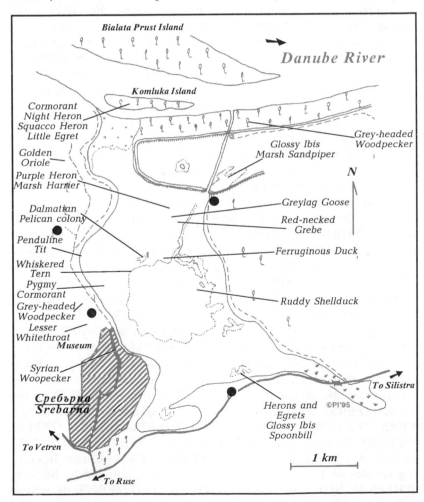

WHITE (some years) EGRETS, PURPLE HERON, SPOONBILL, GLOSSY IBIS, GREYLAG GOOSE, RUDDY SHELDUCK, GADWALL, FERRUGINOUS DUCK (regular in good numbers), BLACK KITE (can be seen flying along the Danube River or on the marsh itself), MARSH HARRIER, CRAKES and RALES, COMMON, BLACK (some years) and WHISKERED TERNS. The site is one with the largest numbers of CUCKOOS which can ever be seen in Bulgaria (of both grey and red phases). The KINGFISHER is common there, the ROLLER and HOOPOE breed in the surroundings of the marsh. There is a very interesting composition of WOODPECKERS around Srebarna: the WRYNECK and SYRIAN WOODPECKER breed in gardens of the village, the BLACK WOODPECKER in trees along the Danube, where the GREY-HEADED WOODPECKER also breeds (but also in solitary trees on the western bank of the marsh), GREEN and LESSER SPOTTED WOODPECKERS are also not rare around. In agricultural fields, it is possible to see the BLACK-HEADED YELLOW WAGTAIL. The rich vegetation keeps good numbers of GREAT REED, MARSH, REED WARBLERS, some SAVI'S and GRASSHOPPER WARBLERS and, given good chance, one can find even the RIVER WARBLER. The BARRED WARBLER can be seen in bushy areas around the wetland. The PENDULINE TIT is a common breeder along the banks, and it is not difficult to observe nests of this interesting bird. The RED-BACKED and sometimes LESSER GREY SHRIKES, BLACK-HEADED and ORTOLAN BUNTINGS and other interesting PASSERINES can be seen easily.

Passage: The area is one of the best for birding during this time along the Danube River. It is possible to see RED-THROATED and BLACK-THROATED DIVERS, almost all European species of GREBES, WHITE PELICANS, WHITE and BLACK STORKS, almost all species of HERONS, many species of DUCKS, and almost all European species of RAPTORS: dozens of HONEY BUZZARDS and LESSER SPOTTED EAGLES, all species of HARRIERS, including the PALLID HARRIER, KITES, all species of HAWKS, some species of EAGLES (the BOOTED, SHORT-TOED, sometimes IMPERIAL and, regularly, the OSPREY) and RED-FOOTED FALCONS, the HOBBY, sometimes the SAKER, and others. COMMON CRANES can also be seen over the site. On the small shallow wetlands between the marsh and the Danube, several species of WADERS stop - some STINTS and SANDPIPERS (including WOOD and MARSH SANDPIPERS), PLOVERS, CURLEWS, GODWITS, SPOTTED REDSHANKS, GREENSHANKS. There, as well as along the banks of the marsh itself, SNIPES and JACK SNIPES, and even GREAT SNIPES can be seen. Interesting species of TERNS can be observed too – CASPIAN, BLACK, WHITE-WINGED BLACK and WHISKERED TERNS, as well as

LITTLE GULLS. BEE-EATERS fly regularly over Srebarna. SWALLOWS and MARTINS, PIPITS, WAGTAILS and other PASSERINES cross the area sometimes in great numbers. In woody and bushy areas, many species of _Sylvia_ and _Phylloscopus_ WARBLERS (including the ICTERINE WARBLER), as well as all species of FLYCATCHERS can be observed.

Winter: The wintering birds of Srebarna include some RED-THROATED and BLACK-THROATED DIVERS, lots of GREBES of different sorts, PYGMY CORMORANTS, DALMATIAN PELICANS (they usually come back to the nests in February), the BITTERN, GREAT WHITE EGRET, some species of GEESE (several thousand WHITE-FRONTED GEESE), but also including the RED-BREASTED GOOSE, many DUCK species, including the GOLDENEYE, SMEW, GOOSANDER, other DIVING DUCKS, sometimes the RED KITE, ROUGH-LEGGED BUZZARD, WHITE-TAILED EAGLE (up to 5 individuals in some winters), also BARN and SHORT-EARED OWLS, some PASSERINES.

Degree of difficulty: Almost all described places require no special effort and are very easy for observing birds by people of any degree of walking ability.

Facilities: _Fuel_: The nearest refilling station is in Silistra (Силистра), which is at 18 km.
Food: Silistra (Силистра) provides many opportunities for different foods. A small coffee bar exist near the museum and a small shop in the centre of the village.
Accommodation: The nearest hotels are in Silistra (Силистра), where different levels of accommodation opportunities (including small private hotels) exist.
Language: Mainly Bulgarian, but there are some people speaking English or other foreign languages at Silistra.

Status: The area of the marsh together with the Komluka Island is a biosphere reserve, Ramsar Site, World Heritage Site and IBA. The banks of the wetland are borders of the protected territory.
Permission: As a reserve, entering Srebarna at any place other than described above needs a written permission from the Ministry of Environment.

Recorder: BSPB HQ.

Aleko
(Алеко)

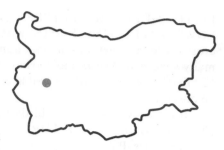

Type: A high-montane area (1 500-2 290 m a.s.l.) of Vitosha (Витоша планина) Mountain. The site includes coniferous forests, mixed with some grassy slopes and a sub-alpine type bushy and stony area around the highest peak of the mountain. Moraines and mountain moorlands and bogs on the plateau, as well as several streams and different buildings complete the mosaic of the habitats of the site.

Location and strategy: The site is situated at about 20 km south of the centre of Sofia (София) and it includes the area of the tourist complex Moreni (Морени) – Stastlivetza (Щастливеца) and mountain hut Aleko (хижа Алеко). There are many ways to reach the site from the city of Sofia. By car follow the road signs to the above-mentioned places, cross the village of Dragalevtzi (Драгалевци) and the end of the road is a car parking near the mountain hut Aleko. The same place can be reached by cabin lift from Simeonovo (Симеоново) or by chair lift from Dragalevtzi (Драгалевци). It is possible to walk to the site along the numerous paths starting from the two mentioned villages and from the village of Bistritza (the path crosses the Bistrishko Branishte Biosphere Reserve (Биосферен резерват Бистришко

Nucifraga caryocatactes

бранище). From the area of the mountain hut Aleko it is possible to walk (on a plain surface) toward the Bistrishko Branishte Biosphere Reserve (Биосферен резерват Бистришко бранище) some 2-3 km to a small bridge across moraines. Another option is to claim the Cherni Vrah peak (Черни връх) by foot (very steep) or by chair lift from Aleko. It is possible to walk from Aleko toward Platoto

(Платото) and Kopitoto (Копитото) to the moorlands and bogs in the plateau area. From all these places you have to walk back along the same or close to the same path. To walk to other mountain huts or areas of Vitosha, use specialised mountain guidebooks or advices of the staff of the mountain service (Планинска контролно-спасителна служба).

Birds: *Breeding birds*: the SPARROWHAWK and GOSHAWKS can be seen virtually at any place of the area except treeless parts. The HONEY BUZZARD can be observed sometimes too. Rarely, the SHORT-TOED EAGLE flies searching for food over the plateau. The peak area is a breeding site of the KESTREL. There are HAZEL GROUSE in the Bistrishko Branishte Biosphere Reserve (Биосферен резерват Бистришко бранище), but to observe them, special efforts (and equipment) are necessary. The GREY PARTRIDGE lives on the plateau. Besides, the WOODPIGEON, STOCK DOVE can be seen rarely. The CUCKOO is quite common. Several species of OWLS exist in the area, but to be seen, a special preparation and the right season are necessary. The LONG-EARED OWL, TAWNY OWL, TENG-MALM'S OWL, SCOPS OWL and LITTLE OWL can be found in different habitats of the site. The BLACK, GREEN and GREAT SPOT-TED WOODPECKERS can be observed for sure. Many other PASSE-

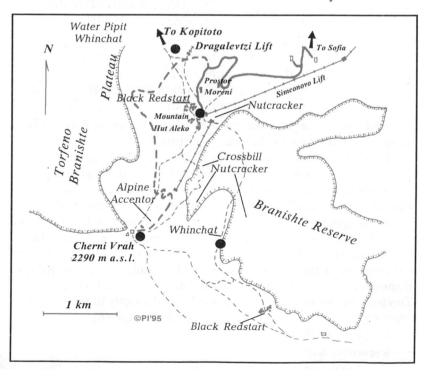

RINES can be seen from short distance at relevant habitats: WOODLARK, SHORE LARK, subspecies *balkanica* (rarely), CRAG MARTIN (near the mountain hut itself), WATER and TREE PIPITS (near the open areas close to subalpine or tree vegetation), GREY WAGTAIL, DIPPER (both along streams), DUNNOCK and ALPINE ACCENTOR (numerous in the bushy and stony areas close to the peak), BLACK REDSTART (abundant), WHINCHAT (common in high grassy areas), ROCK THRUSH, RING OUZEL (common in the high-montane coniferous forest), SONG and MISTLE THRUSHES, WOOD WARBLER, GOLDCREST and FIRECREST, MARSH, WILLOW and CRESTED TITS, TREECREEPER, RED-BACKED SHRIKE, NUT-CRACKER (very common in the forest area, including close to the mountain hut itself), RAVEN, SERIN, SISKIN, BULLFINCH, LINNET, CROSSBILL, YELLOWHAMMER, ROCK BUNTING.

Passage: Mainly PASSERINES, and especially prominent are waves of the SWALLOWS and MARTINS, PIPITS, LEAF and *SYLVIA* WARBLERS, all European species of FLYCATCHERS, some SHRIKES.

Winter: Good opportunities to see from close distance and without special efforts several species of WOODPECKERS, SHORE LARK, ALPINE ACCENTOR, RING OUZEL, GOLDCREST, FIRECREST, CRESTED TIT, WALLCREEPER (not easy to see this species despite its permanent presence in the area during this period), NUTCRACKER (feeding from the litter boxes near buildings), CROSSBILLS, and others.

Degree of difficulty: There are many possibilities for shorter or longer walks around the place along the paths, some very easy, other quite difficult and requiring special preparations, but the most interesting birds can be seen just from the path.

Facilities: *Fuel*: The nearest possibilities to obtain it are in Sofia (about 15 km to some of the nearest stations).

Food: There is an extremely rich choice for obtaining different foods — from different sorts of restaurants to food shops all year round.

Accommodation: There are many different level hotels both in and around the area, including the villages at the foothills of Vitosha Mountain.

Language: Mainly Bulgarian, but it is possible to find many people speaking English or other foreign languages, especially in the tourist area.

Status: All Vitosha Mountain is a National Park. There are several reserves, including the Bistrishko Branishte Biosphere Reserve (Биосферен резерват Бистришко branище), Torfeno Branishte (Торфено branище), where access is limited strictly to marked paths under control of the Park administration and some volunteers.

Permission: Not required.

Recorder: BSPB HQ.

Dragoman Marsh and Chepan Hill (Драгоманско блато и хълма Чепън)

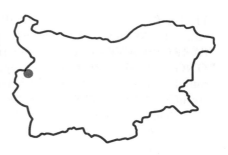

Type: Remains of a large marsh on the Sofia Plain near the town of Dragoman and calcareous hills with some vertical and close-to-vertical rocks, with bushes and high grasses. The marsh remains are represented by some small water bodies, covered with marsh vegetation, and by several drainage canals. In some years the marshland dries up almost completely and becomes devoid of breeding water birds. The marshland area is surrounded from the other sides by agricultural fields and wet meadows.

Location and strategy: The site is situated near international road E80 and is about 5 km east of the town of Dragoman (Драгоман), near the asphalt road from Dragoman (Драгоман) to Golemo Malovo (Големо Малово). The easiest way is to turn to the east from the road junction near Dragoman (Драгоман), to stop near the road at the foothills of Chepan near a small pump station, and to watch from that place. It is possible to walk from it towards the remains of the marsh (southward) or towards the hill itself (do not walk more than 100 - 150 m because of a possible disturbance of birds). For CORN-CRAKES, it is necessary to travel several kilometers further, where in the wet meadows, especially between the villages of Golemo Malovo (Големо Малово) and Malo Malovo (Мало Малово), during the night (sometimes during the day too), it is possible to hear calling birds just from the road.

Birds: *Breeding birds* of the site include the LITTLE GREBE,

Buteo rufinus

LITTLE BITTERN, WHITE STORK (breeding in the settlements around), MARSH HARRIER (some years), GOSHAWK, SPARROWHAWK (birds coming from the forests in the region), LONG-LEGGED BUZZARD (regular over the slopes and plain around), QUAIL, some CRAKES and RALES, including good numbers of CORNCRAKES, LAPWING, HOOPOE, LITTLE OWL (in the settlements around), BLACK-HEADED YELLOW WAGTAIL (in agricultural fields), BLACK REDSTART, STONECHAT, ROCK TRUSH (all on rocky slopes), GREAT REED, MARSH and REED WARBLERS, LESSER WHITETHROAT, BARRED WARBLER, RED-BACKED SHRIKE, CORN, CIRL, ORTOLAN, and ROCK BUNTINGS.

Passage: The area is one of the best for birding during this time in the Sofia Plain. It is possible to see almost all European species of GREBES, the PYGMY CORMORANT (rarely), WHITE and BLACK STORKS, almost all species of HERONS, the GLOSSY IBIS and SPOONBILL, some GEESE species (the GREYLAG and the WHITE-FRONTED GOOSE), many species of DUCKS: the SHELLDUCK, WIGEON, GADWALL, PINTAIL, SHOVELER, TEAL, GARGANEY, POCHARD, FERRUGINOUS DUCK, TUFTED DUCK, and others. The fact that the site is situated on a migratory route, at the same time connected with the Struma Valley (Via Aristotelis), is the reason to see almost all European RAPTORS flying individually or in small groups: the BLACK KITE, EGYPTIAN VULTURE, all species of HARRIERS and HAWKS, the HONEY BUZZARD, LESSER SPOTTED,

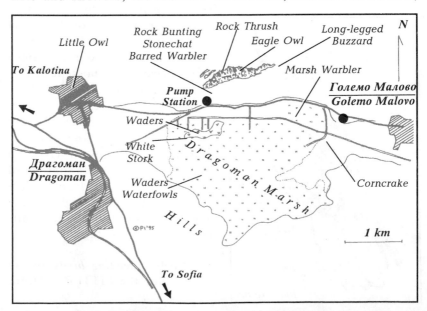

BOOTED, SHORT-TOED EAGLES, the OSPREY, RED-FOOTED
FALCON, LESSER KESTREL, HOBBY, PEREGRINE, and others.
The COMMON CRANE (for which the marsh is a former breeding
place) can also be seen over the site. On small shallow wetlands, several species of WADERS stop during this period. BLACK-WINGED
STILTS, PLOVERS, SANDPIPERS and STINTS (including WOOD
and MARSH SANDPIPERS), RUFFS, CURLEWS, GODWITS, RED-
SHANKS, SPOTTED REDSHANKS, GREENSHANKS. The site is
exellent for the SNIPES, JACK SNIPES and, more rarely, for GREAT
SNIPES. Some species of GULLS and TERNS can be observed too,
including BLACK, WHITE-WINGED BLACK and WHISKERED
TERNS. BEE-EATERS are regular migrants. The NIGHTJAR can be
seen in the woody areas around. SWALLOWS and MARTINS, PIP-
ITS, WAGTAILS, WHINCHATS and STONECHATS, different species of WHEATEARS, WARBLERS, FLYCATCHERS, SHRIKES,
FINCHES and BUNTINGS can be observed.

Winter: The wintering birds of the area include some GREAT
WHITE EGRETS, some species of GEESE (mainly WHITE-FRONTED
GEESE flying over the marsh), some DUCK species, during colder
winters the ROUGH-LEGGED BUZZARD, SHORT-EARED OWL,
some PASSERINES.

Degree of difficulty: Almost all described places do not require
any special effort and are very easy for observing birds by people of
any degree of walking ability.

Facilities:*Fuel*: The nearest station is in Dragoman (Драгоман),
which is at about 5 km.

Food: Dragoman (Драгоман) provides some opportunities for
different foods. Several cafe bars exist along the international road.

Accommodation: The nearest hotels are in Dragoman (Драгоман),
where different options for accommodation (including small private
hotels) exist.

Language: Mainly Bulgarian, but along the international road it
is possible to find people speaking English or other foreign languages.

Status: No special statute.
Permission: No limitations for walking in the area, but claiming
the hill is not recommended because of disturbance of some birds.
Recorder: BSPB HQ.

9

Kresna
(Кресна)

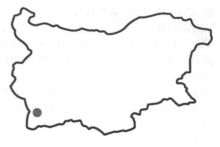

Type: A relatively narrow valley of Struma River (река Струма) near the town of Kresna (Кресна). A middle-sized river bed with meanders between dry stony hills turning northward into a deep valley with high cliffs. There is a mixture of habitats, including river bank vegetation, large areas with a mediterranean type of vegetation, consisting of dry grasses, evergreen bushes (*Taxus baccata, Juniperus oxycedris*, etc.), mixed with low trees, some forested areas and rocky and stony slopes, relatively small agricultural fields, pastures, and several villages and towns around.

Location and strategy: The town of Kresna (Кресна) is situated about 45 km north of the cross-border with Greece at Kulata (Кулата), on road E79. One of the starting points is the town, from which it is possible to walk to the areas around, mainly along the Struma River and to the hills with mediterranean vegetation. A very interesting place is a stony wall near the southeastern end of the town, called Melo (Мело), where the ROCK SPARROW breeds. There are wet meadows between Melo and the railway station, where interesting birds can be seen too. Also, many places along the road to the north of the town of Kresna provide good opportunities to stop and observe birds from the place or during short walks around. Following E79, it is possible to get to Gara Peyu Yavorov (Гара Пею Яворов), the surroundings of which also offer excellent birding. A good place is also the Kresnensko Hanche complex (Кресненско ханче). Another opportunity is to take a road to the village of Gorna Breznitza (Горна Брезница) and to make observations along it.

Monticola solitarius

Birds: *Breeding birds.* The LONG-LEGGED BUZZARD, GOLDEN and SHORT-TOED EAGLES, HOBBY and PEREGRINE are the most probable RAPTORS to be observed over the valley. On the river bed, the LITTLE RINGED PLOVER can be found at the end of the summer. The EAGLE, SCOPS and LITTLE OWLS and the NIGHTJAR can be heard or seen in the area too. The ALPINE SWIFT, KINGFISHER, HOOPOE, SYRIAN WOODPECKER are other possible birds. Among the PASSERINES, the most interesting are 'mediterranean' species: the BLUE ROCK THRUSH, ROCK THRUSH, SUBALPINE, BARRED, SARDINIAN, ORPHEAN and OLIVE-TREE WARBLERS, the SOMBRE TIT, ROCK NUTHATCH, MASKED

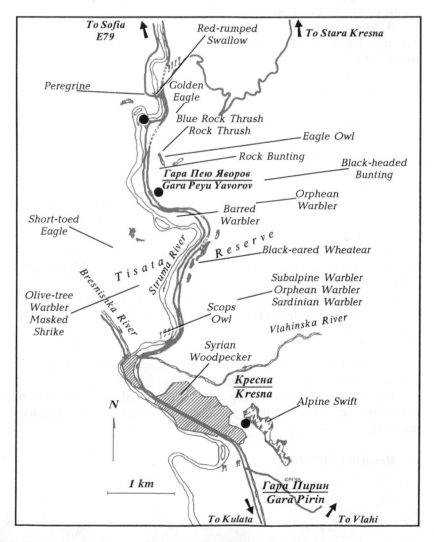

SHRIKE, ROCK SPARROW, ROCK and BLACK-HEADED BUN-
TINGS. This is one of the places, where the ITALIAN SPARROW can
be seen in Bulgaria. In the wet meadow near the railway station, GREAT
REED and MARSH WARBLERS can be observed.

Passage: The Struma valley is a quite busy migrating route of birds
(Via Aristotelis). The Kresna area is no exception. Many species of HER-
ONS and EGRETS, sometimes BLACK and WHITE STORKS, almost
all species of RAPTORS use the river, the vertical air flows of surrounding hills or vegetation on the banks during the migration period. Very
abundant are PASSERINES, including SEMI-COLLARED and PIED
FLYCATCHERS, some LEAF WARBLERS and other species which are
almost everywhere on passage.

Winter: Wintering GREEN SANDPIPERS can be seen along the
river together with the resident KINGFISHERS and some other birds,
mainly PASSERINES.

Degree of difficulty: Most of the described birds can be seen just
from the road or from easy paths and old sectors of the road along the
river. In general, the area is easy for almost all people regardless of
their walking abilities.

Facilities: *Fuel*: The town of Kresna (Кресна) is the nearest place
to obtain it.

Food: There are some opportunities to get food in the area, mainly
in Kresna (Кресна), but it is better to get supplied in advance with
food and drinks for a stay at the site.

Accommodation: The nearest hotels are in Kresna (Кресна), but
for a better accommodation it is necessary to travel to Blagoevgrad
(41 km northward).

Language: Almost no people speaking English or other foreign
languages in the settlements. Only along the E79 road some people
speak foreign languages.

Status: Part of the area (the bushy area covered with *Taxus
baccata*) is a reserve, called Tisata (резерват Тисата).

Permission: To walk in the areas with a mediterranean type of
vegetation, you need a written permission from the Ministry of Environment.

Recorder: BSPB HQ.

Rupite
(Рупите)

Type: An open valley of Struma River (река Струма) near the village of Rupite (Рупите). An interesting mixture of habitats, including a middle-size river, some marshland areas and fish ponds along the banks, forested areas and such with a mediterranean type of vegetation, rocky and stony slopes and cliffs on the surrounding hills and on the slopes of the extinct Volkano Kozhukh (Кожух). Riverine vegetation, agricultural lands and several villages and towns around complete the picture.

Location and strategy: The village of Rupite (Рупите) is situated about 7 km north of the town of Petrich (Петрич) and about 25 km from Kulata (Кулата), the cross-border point with Greece, on international road E79. One good site is a small marsh at the place where the road to Petrich (Петрич) from the road-junction south of the village of Novo Delchevo (Ново Делчево) crosses the railway. Another very good place is the fish farm near the bridge across Struma River west of the previous place. It is possible to drive or walk about a kilometre along a cart-road which is near the pools of the fish farm. Following the asphalt road to Petrich (Петрич) some 5 km after the bridge at a relatively sharp right turn, there is a crossroads to Rupite (Рупите). It is possible to leave the car in a parking close to the new Church of Vanga (Църквата на баба Ванга) and to make some walk to the foothills or slopes of the Kozhukh Volcano (вулкана Кожух). A good viewing place is also the hill north of the village of General Todorov (Генерал Тодоров). Walk from the village northward along the railway and on a well visible path you will claim a rocky hill with a small chapel called St. Panteleimon (Параклис Св. Пантелеймон), where there is a good view of the valley.

Sitta neumayer

Birds: *Breeding birds.* The LITTLE GREBE and LITTLE BIT-
TERN breed some years on some of the wetlands with stagnant
water, the WHITE STORK can be seen on the nest in villages, the
EGYPTIAN VULTURE can be seen sometimes flying over the area.
The GOSHAWK is a regular breeder, but also the LEVANT
SPARROWHAWK occurs in the region. From the other RAPTORS,
the HONEY BUZZARD, LONG-LEGGED BUZZARD, SHORT-
TOED, BOOTED and LESSER-SPOTTED EAGLES, HOBBY,
LESSER and COMMON KESTRELS, as well as non-breeding
ELEONORA'S FALCON (occasionally) can be observed over the
valley. The LITTLE RINGED PLOVER and STONE-CURLEW

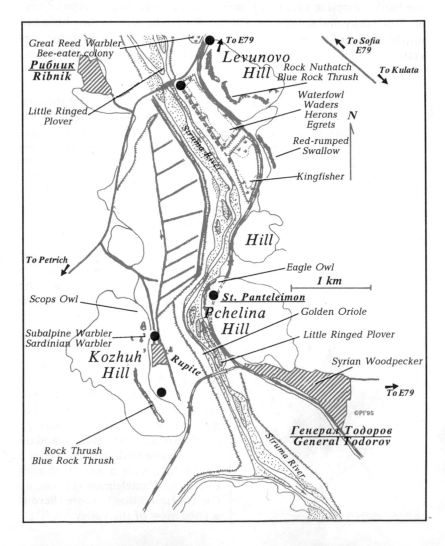

breed on the Struma River bed. The EAGLE, SCOPS and LITTLE OWLS, NIGHTJAR exist there. The KINGFISHER, BEE-EATER, ROLLER and HOOPOE, SYRIAN and MIDDLE SPOTTED WOODPECKERS can be observed. From among PASSERINES, most interesting are the TAWNY PIPIT, CRAG MARTIN, RED-RUMPED SWALLOW, BLUE ROCK THRUSH and ROCK THRUSH, SUBALPINE, BARRED, SARDINIAN, ORPHEAN, BONELLI'S and OLIVE-TREE WARBLERS, SOMBRE TIT, ROCK NUTHATCH, MASKED SHRIKE, ROCK SPARROW, ROCK and BLACK-HEADED BUNTINGS, etc.

Passage: After the Black Sea coast, the Struma Valley is one of the most busy migrating routes of birds over Bulgaria. It is well-known from ancient times as Via Aristotelis. Being situated there, Rupite is a site with a very rich migrating bird fauna. Almost all species of GREBES, CORMORANTS, HERONS and EGRETS, small flocks of BLACK and WHITE STORKS, GLOSSY IBIS, GEESE and DUCKS (including the globally threatened LESSER WHITE-FRONTED GOOSE), almost all species of RAPTORS fly over the river or use vegetation on the banks for roosting. The COMMON, MARSH and GREEN SANDPIPER, WOODCOCK, SNIPE and JACK SNIPE, as well as several species of GULLS and TERNS, including MARSH TERNS, use the river valley and ponds during migration. Large numbers of PASSERINES, including SEMI-COLLARED and PIED FLY-CATCHERS, some LEAF WARBLERS are quite common on passage.

Winter: Fishing PYGMY CORMORANTS and GREAT WHITE EGRETS can be seen on the river and some other wetlands. The same habitat supports some WATERFOWL. The usual mild winter weather in the area provides favourable conditions for many birds of other species, especially PASSERINES.

Degree of difficulty: Most of the described birds can be seen just from the road, but there are many possibilities for short walks around the river along paths. Some of the walks in the hills are more difficult. In general, the area is easy for almost all people regardless of their walking abilities.

Facilities: *Fuel*: Petrich (Петрич), at 7 km, and Kulata (Кулата), at about 25 km, are the nearest possibilities to obtain it.

Food: There are many opportunities to get food in the area, mainly in towns, but it is better to get supplied in advance with food and drinks for a stay at the site.

Accommodation: The nearest hotels are in Petrich (Петрич), at about 7 km. Some possibilities for accommodation exist in the village of Rupite itself, which is a place with hot mineral springs, but because of high interest to it, they are not sure.

Language: Almost no people speaking English or other foreign languages. Only along the E79 road and at Petrich (Петрич), some people speak foreign languages.

Status: No special statute.

Permission: Not required. The area is open to the public.

Recorder: BSPB HQ.

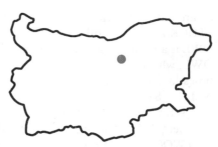

Veliko Tarnovo
(Велико Търново)

Type: A part of the valley of Yantra River (река Янтра) north of Veliko Tarnovo (Велико Търново), with limestone cliffs along the slopes on both sides of the valley. Parts of the slopes are covered by broad-leaved forests, some areas are with dry grasses and scrubs. The area includes riverine vegetation and sandy, shingle and stony sectors of the bed of Yantra River, some small agricultural lands and the built-up areas of several villages and towns around, including the old Bulgarian capital - Veliko Tarnovo. Two famous Bulgarian monasteries: Preobrazhenski Monastery (Преображенски манастир) and Sveta Troitza Monastery (Манастир Света Троица) are situated near the rock walls on the top of both sides of the valley.

Location and strategy: The site is situated north of the town of Veliko Tarnovo (Велико Търново) along the road E85 to Ruse. Some interesting birds can be seen in the town itself or in the nearby village of Arbanasi (Арбанаси), which is also a very interesting example of Bulgarian architecture (SCOPS and LITTLE OWL, SYRIAN WOOD-PECKER). Another good place to see birds is Preobrazhenski Monastery (Преображенски манастир), to which it is possible to drive on a well-signed asphalt road. The Sveta Troitza Monastery (Манастир Света Троица) is another good site, to which another asphalt road is available. There are many places where it is possible to stop near the road and to watch birds along the river.

Bubo bubo

Birds: *Breeding birds.* The BLACK STORK can be seen over the valley or hills in the western part of the valley, the EGYPTIAN VULTURE and LONG-LEGGED BUZZARD can be observed flying along cliffs, the GOSHAWK and SPARROWHAWK in forested areas or around settlements, sometimes also the HOBBY appears there. The STOCK DOVE is another bird which can be seen in the area. The EAGLE OWL is a resident bird breeding on cliffs, as well as SCOPS and LITTLE OWL, which are more common in settlements. The NIGHTJAR sometimes catches insects around lamps in the suburbs of Veliko Tarnovo. The ALPINE SWIFT and HOOPOE are common birds in the areas with cliffs. The WRYNECK, GREEN and LESSER SPOTTED WOODPECKERS represent their group in parkland areas and along the river and the SYRIAN WOODPECKER in villages and towns. The RED-RUMPED SWALLOW can be seen around rocks, where at some places also the WOODLARK occurs. The GREY WAGTAIL can be seen in the areas with stones along the river, also the CIRL BUNTING can be observed there.

Passage: Many species of RAPTORS, including HARRIERS, BLACK KITE, HOBBY, and others, follow the valley during migration. Flocks of BEE-EATERS regularly fly along the valley during both

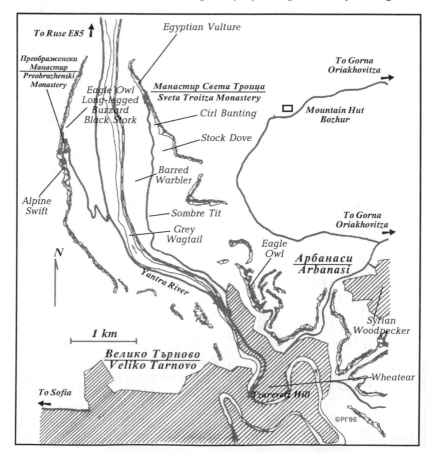

spring and autumn migration. Many PASSERINES, including COL-LARED, SEMI-COLLARED and PIED FLYCATCHERS, STONECHAT, WHINCHAT, some LEAF WARBLERS are quite common on passage.

Winter: The GOSHAWK and SPARROWHAWK, GREEN SAND-PIPER, many PASSERINES, including HAWFINCHES, CORN and CIRL BUNTINGS, are among the most common birds which can be seen in winter.

Degree of difficulty: Most of the described birds can be observed just from the road, but there are many possibilities for short walks. Easy to almost all people regardless of their walking abilities.

Facilities: *Fuel*: The nearest possibilities to obtain it are in Veliko Tarnovo (Велико Търново).

Food: There are many opportunities to have different foods and drinks, including typical examples of traditional Bulgarian meals in Veliko Tarnovo (Велико Търново), Arbanasi (Арбанаси), or in some of the road-by restaurants.

Accommodation: There are many opportunities to be accommodated in different level hotels in Veliko Tarnovo (Велико Търново).

Language: There are some people in the area which speak English or other foreign languages.

Status: No special statute.

Permission: Not required. The area is open to the public. It is not recommended to claim the hills toward the rock faces in order to avoid disturbance of some larger birds there.

Recorder: BSPB HQ.

Index of the English names of birds

List
of Bulgarian
Birds

List of Bulgarian Birds

№	Scientific name	English vernacular name	Bulgarian vernacular name	Your language name
1.	*Gavia stellata*	Red-throated Diver	Червеногуш гмуркач	
2.	*Gavia arctica*	Black-throated Diver	Черногуш гмуркач	
3.	*Gavia immer*	Great Northern Diver	Черноклюн гмуркач	
4.	*Tachybaptus ruficollis*	Little Grebe	Малък гмурец	
5.	*Podiceps cristatus*	Great Crested Grebe	Голям гмурец	
6.	*Podiceps grisegena*	Red-necked Grebe	Червеноврат гмурец	
7.	*Podiceps auritus*	Slavonian Grebe	Ушат гмурец	
8.	*Podiceps nigricollis*	Black-necked Grebe	Черноврат гмурец	
9.	*Calonectris diomedea*	Cory's Shearwater	Жълтоклюн буревестник	
10.	*Puffinus yelkouan*	Yelkouan Shearwater	Обикновен буревестник	
11.	*Hydrobates pelagicus*	British Storm-petrel	Вълнолюбка	
12.	*Morus bassanus*	Gannet	Бял рибояд	
13.	*Phalacrocorax carbo*	Cormorant	Голям корморан	
14.	*Phalacrocorax aristotelis*	Shag	Качулат корморан	
15.	*Phalacrocorax pygmeus*	Pygmy Cormorant	Малък корморан	
16.	*Pelecanus onocrotalus*	White Pelican	Розов пеликан	
17.	*Pelecanus crispus*	Dalmatian Pelican	Къдроглав пеликан	
18.	*Botaurus stellaris*	Bittern	Голям воден бик	
19.	*Ixobrychus minutus*	Little Bittern	Малък воден бик	
20.	*Nycticorax nycticorax*	Night Heron	Нощна чапла	
21.	*Ardeola ralloides*	Squacco Heron	Гривеста чапла	
22.	*Bubulcus ibis*	Cattle Egret	Биволска чапла	
23.	*Egretta garzetta*	Little Egret	Малка бяла чапла	

24.	*Egretta alba*	Great White Egret	Голяма бяла чапла	
25.	*Ardea cinerea*	Grey Heron	Сива чапла	
26.	*Ardea purpurea*	Purple Heron	Червена чапла	
27.	*Ciconia nigra*	Black Stork	Черен щъркел	
28.	*Ciconia ciconia*	White Stork	Бял щъркел	
29.	*Plegadis falcinellus*	Glossy Ibis	Блестящ ибис	
30.	*Platalea leucorodia*	Spoonbill	Бял лопатар	
31.	*Phoenicopterus ruber*	Greater Flamingo	Розово фламинго	
32.	*Cygnus olor*	Mute Swan	Ням лебед	
33.	*(Cygnus atratus)*	Australian Black Swan	Черен лебед	
34.	*Cygnus columbianus*	Bewick's Swan	Тундров лебед	
35.	*Cygnus cygnus*	Whooper Swan	Поен лебед	
36.	*Anser fabalis*	Bean Goose	Посевна гъска	
37.	*Anser albifrons*	White-fronted Goose	Голяма белочела гъска	
38.	*Anser erythropus*	Lesser White-fronted Goose	Малка белочела гъска	
39.	*Anser anser*	Greylag Goose	Сива гъска	
40.	*Anser caerulescens*	Snow Goose	Снежна гъска	
41.	*(Branta canadensis)*	Canada Goose	Канадска гъска	
42.	*Branta bernicla*	Brent Goose	Черна гъска	
43.	*Branta ruficollis*	Red-breasted Goose	Червеногуша гъска	
44.	*Tadorna ferruginea*	Ruddy Shelduck	Червен ангъч	
45.	*Tadorna tadorna*	Shelduck	Бял ангъч	
46.	*(Aix sponsa)*	Wood Duck	Каролинка	
47.	*(Aix galericulata)*	Mandarin Duck	Мандаринка	
48.	*Anas penelope*	Wigeon	Фиш	
49.	*Anas falcata*	Falcated Duck	Сърпокрила патица	

50. *Anas strepera*	Gadwall	Сива патица	
51. *Anas crecca*	Teal	Зимно бърне	
52. *Anas platyrhynchos*	Mallard	Зеленоглава патица	
53. *Anas acuta*	Pintail	Шилоопашата патица	
54. *Anas querquedula*	Garganey	Лятно бърне	
55. *Anas clypeata*	Shoveler	Клопач	
56. *Marmaronetta angustirostris*	Marbled Duck	Мраморна патица	
57. *Netta rufina*	Red-crested Pochard	Червеноклюна потапница	
58. *Aythya ferina*	Pochard	Кафявоглава потапница	
59. *Aythya nyroca*	Ferruginous Duck	Белоока потапница	
60. *Aythya fuligula*	Tufted Duck	Качулата потапница	
61. *Aythya marila*	Scaup	Планинска потапница	
62. *Somateria mollissima*	Eider	Гага	
63. *Clangula hyemalis*	Long-tailed Duck	Ледена потапница	
64. *Melanitta nigra*	Common Scoter	Траурна потапница	
65. *Melanitta fusca*	Velvet Scoter	Кадифена потапница	
66. *Bucephala clangula*	Goldeneye	Звънарка	
67. *(Mergus cucullatus)*	Hooded Merganser	Качулат нирец	
68. *Mergus albellus*	Smew	Малък нирец	
69. *Mergus serrator*	Red-breasted Merganser	Среден нирец	
70. *Mergus merganser*	Goosander	Голям нирец	
71. *Oxyura leucocephala*	White-headed Duck	Тръноопашата потапница	
72. *Pernis apivorus*	Honey Buzzard	Осояд	
73. *Elanus caeruleus*	Black-shouldered Kite	Пепелява каня	
74. *Milvus migrans*	Black Kite	Черна каня	
75. *Milvus milvus*	Red Kite	Червена каня	

76. *Haliaeetus albicilla*	White-tailed Eagle	Морски орел	
77. *Gypaetus barbatus*	Lammergeier	Брадат лешояд	
78. *Neophron percnopterus*	Egyptian Vulture	Египетски лешояд	
79. *Gyps fulvus*	Griffon Vulture	Белоглав лешояд	
80. *Aegypius monachus*	Black Vulture	Черен лешояд	
81. *Circaetus gallicus*	Short-toed Eagle	Орел змияр	
82. *Circus aeruginosus*	Marsh Harrier	Тръстиков блатар	
83. *Circus cyaneus*	Hen Harrier	Полски блатар	
84. *Circus macrourus*	Pallid Harrier	Степен блатар	
85. *Circus pygargus*	Montagu's Harrier	Ливаден блатар	
86. *Accipiter gentilis*	Goshawk	Голям ястреб	
87. *Accipiter nisus*	Sparrowhawk	Малък ястреб	
88. *Accipiter brevipes*	Levant Sparrowhawk	Късопръст ястреб	
89. *Buteo buteo*	Buzzard	Обикновен мишелов	
90. *Buteo rufinus*	Long-legged Buzzard	Белоопашат мишелов	
91. *Buteo lagopus*	Rough-legged Buzzard	Северен мишелов	
92. *Aquila pomarina*	Lesser Spotted Eagle	Малък креслив орел	
93. *Aquila clanga*	Spotted Eagle	Голям креслив орел	
94. *Aquila nipalensis*	Steppe Eagle	Степен орел	
95. *Aquila heliaca*	Imperial Eagle	Царски орел	
96. *Aquila chrysaetos*	Golden Eagle	Скален орел	
97. *Hieraaetus pennatus*	Booted Eagle	Малък орел	
98. *Hieraaetus fasciatus*	Bonelli's Eagle	Ястребов орел	
99. *Pandion haliaetus*	Osprey	Речен орел	
100. *Falco naumanni*	Lesser Kestrel	Белошипа ветрушка	
101. *Falco tinnunculus*	Kestrel	Черношипа ветрушка	

102.	*Falco vespertinus*	Red-footed Falcon	Червенонога ветрушка	
103.	*Falco columbarius*	Merlin	Малък сокол	
104.	*Falco subbuteo*	Hobby	Орко	
105.	*Falco eleonorae*	Eleonora's Falcon	Средиземноморски сокол	
106.	*Falco biarmicus*	Lanner	Далматински сокол	
107.	*Falco cherrug*	Saker	Ловен сокол	
108.	*Falco peregrinus*	Peregrine	Сокол скитник	
109.	*Bonasa bonasia*	Hazel Grouse	Лещарка	
110.	*Tetrao tetrix*∗	Black Grouse	Тетрев	
111.	*Tetrao urogallus*	Capercaillie	Глухар	
112.	*Alectoris chukar*	Chukar	Тракийски кеклик	
113.	*Alectoris graeca*	Rock Partridge	Планински кеклик	
114.	*Perdix perdix*	Grey Partridge	Яребица	
115.	*Coturnix coturnix*	Quail	Пъдпъдък	
116.	*Phasianus colchicus*	Pheasant	Колхидски фазан	
117.	*Rallus aquaticus*	Water Rail	Крещалец	
118.	*Porzana porzana*	Spotted Crake	Голяма пъструшка	
119.	*Porzana parva*	Little Crake	Средна пъструшка	
120.	*Porzana pusilla*	Baillon's Crake	Малка пъструшка	
121.	*Crex crex*	Corncrake	Ливаден дърдавец	
122.	*Gallinula chloropus*	Moorhen	Зеленоножка	
123.	*Fulica atra*	Coot	Лиска	
124.	*Grus grus*	Crane	Сив жерав	
125.	*Anthropoides virgo*	Demoiselle Crane	Момин жерав	
126.	*Tetrax tetrax*	Little Bustard	Стрепет	
127.	*Otis tarda*	Great Bustard	Дропла	

156

128. *Haematopus ostralegus*	Oystercatcher	Стридояд	
129. *Himantopus himantopus*	Black-winged Stilt	Кокилобегач	
130. *Recurvirostra avosetta*	Avocet	Саблеклюн	
131. *Burhinus oedicnemus*	Stone-curlew	Турилик	
132. *Glareola pratincola*	Collared Pratincole	Кафявокрил огърличник	
133. *Glareola nordmanni*	Black-winged Pratincole	Чернокрил огърличник	
134. *Charadrius dubius*	Little Ringed Plover	Речен дъждосвирец	
135. *Charadrius hiaticula*	Ringed Plover	Пясъчен дъждосвирец	
136. *Charadrius alexandrinus*	Kentish Plover	Морски дъждосвирец	
137. *Charadrius leschenaultii*	Greater Sand Plover	Дългокрак дъждосвирец	
138. *Charadrius asiaticus*	Caspian Plover	Каспийски дъждосвирец	
139. *Charadrius morinellus*	Dotterel	Планински дъждосвирец	
140. *Pluvialis apricaria*	Golden Plover	Златиста булка	
141. *Pluvialis squatarola*	Grey Plover	Сребриста булка	
142. *Hoplopterus spinosus*	Spur-winged Plover	Шипокрила калугерица	
143. *Chettusia gregaria*	Sociable Plover	Степна калугерица	
144. *Vanellus vanellus*	Lapwing	Обикновена калугерица	
145. *Calidris canutus*	Knot	Голям брегобегач	
146. *Calidris alba*	Sanderling	Трипръст брегобегач	
147. *Calidris minuta*	Little Stint	Малък брегобегач	
148. *Calidris temminckii*	Temminck's Stint	Сив брегобегач	
149. *Calidris ferruginea*	Curlew Sandpiper	Кривоклюн брегобегач	
150. *Calidris alpina*	Dunlin	Тъмногръд брегобегач	
151. *Limicola falcinellus*	Broad-billed Sandpiper	Плоскоклюн брегобегач	
152. *Tryngites subruficollis*	Buff-breasted Sandpiper	Ръждивогръд брегобегач	
153. *Philomachus pugnax*	Ruff	Бойник	

154.	*Lymnocryptes minimus*	Jack Snipe	Малка бекасина
155.	*Gallinago gallinago*	Snipe	Средна бекасина
156.	*Gallinago media*	Great Snipe	Голяма бекасина
157.	*Scolopax rusticola*	Woodcock	Горски бекас
158.	*Limosa limosa*	Black-tailed Godwit	Черноопашат крайбрежен бекас
159.	*Limosa lapponica*	Bar-tailed Godwit	Пъстроопашат крайбрежен бекас
160.	*Numenius phaeopus*	Whimbrel	Малък свирец
161.	*Numenius tenuirostris*	Slender-billed Curlew	Тънкоклюн свирец
162.	*Numenius arquata*	Curlew	Голям свирец
163.	*Tringa erythropus*	Spotted Redshank	Голям червеноног водобегач
164.	*Tringa totanus*	Redshank	Малък червеноног водобегач
165.	*Tringa stagnatilis*	Marsh Sandpiper	Малък зеленоног водобегач
166.	*Tringa nebularia*	Greenshank	Голям зеленоног водобегач
167.	*Tringa ochropus*	Green Sandpiper	Голям горски водобегач
168.	*Tringa glareola*	Wood Sandpiper	Малък горски водобегач
169.	*Xenus cinereus*	Terek Sandpiper	Пепеляв брегобегач
170.	*Actitis hypoleucos*	Common Sandpiper	Късокрил кюкавец
171.	*Actitis macularia*	Spotted Sandpiper	Петнист кюкавец
172.	*Arenaria interpres*	Turnstone	Камъкообръщач
173.	*Phalaropus lobatus*	Red-necked Phalarope	Тънкоклюн листоног
174.	*Phalaropus fulicarius*	Grey Phalarope	Плоскоклюн листоног
175.	*Stercorarius pomarinus*	Pomarine Skua	Голям морелетник
176.	*Stercorarius parasiticus*	Arctic Skua	Среден морелетник
177.	*Stercorarius longicaudus*	Long-tailed Skua	Дългоопашат морелетник
178.	*Stercorarius skua*	Great Skua	Скуа
179.	*Larus ichthyaetus*	Great Black-headed Gull	Голяма черноглава чайка

180.	*Larus relictus*	Relict Gull	Реликтна чайка	
181.	*Larus melanocephalus*	Mediterranean Gull	Малка черноглава чайка	
182.	*Larus minutus*	Little Gull	Малка чайка	
183.	*Larus sabini*	Sabine's Gull	Вилоопашата чайка	
184.	*Larus ridibundus*	Black-headed Gull	Речна чайка	
185.	*Larus genei*	Slender-billed Gull	Дългоклюна чайка	
186.	*Larus delawarensis*	Ring-billed Gull	Пръстенчатоклюна чайка	
187.	*Larus canus*	Common Gull	Чайка буревестница	
188.	*Larus fuscus*	Lesser Black-backed Gull	Малка черногърба чайка	
189.	*Larus argentatus*	Herring Gull	Сребриста чайка	
190.	*Larus cachinnans*	Yellow-legged Gull	Жълтокрака чайка	
191.	*Larus marinus*	Great Black-backed Gull	Голяма черногърба чайка	
192.	*Rissa tridactyla*	Kittiwake	Трипръста чайка	
193.	*Gelochelidon nilotica*	Gull-billed Tern	Дебелоклюна рибарка	
194.	*Sterna caspia*	Caspian Tern	Каспийска рибарка	
195.	*Sterna sandvicensis*	Sandwich Tern	Гривеста рибарка	
196.	*Sterna hirundo*	Common Tern	Речна рибарка	
197.	*Sterna paradisaea*	Arctic Tern	Полярна рибарка	
198.	*Sterna albifrons*	Little Tern	Малка рибарка	
199.	*Chlidonias hybridus*	Whiskered Tern	Белобуза рибарка	
200.	*Chlidonias niger*	Black Tern	Черна рибарка	
201.	*Chlidonias leucopterus*	White-winged Black Tern	Белокрила рибарка	
202.	*Uria aalge*	Guillemot	Тънкоклюна кайра	
203.	*Syrrhaptes paradoxus*	Pallas's Sandgrouse	Пухопръста пустинарка	
204.	*Columba livia*	Rock Dove	Див скален гълъб	
205.	*Columba oenas*	Stock Dove	Гълъб хралупар	

162

206.	*Columba palumbus*	Woodpigeon	Гривяк	
207.	*(Streptopelia roseogrisea)*	African Collared Dove	Смехурка	
208.	*Streptopelia decaocto*	Collared Dove	Гугутка	
209.	*Streptopelia turtur*	Turtle Dove	Гургулица	
210.	*Clamator glandarius*	Great Spotted Cuckoo	Качулата кукувица	
211.	*Cuculus canorus*	Cuckoo	Обикновена кукувица	
212.	*Tyto alba*	Barn Owl	Забулена сова	
213.	*Otus scops*	Scops Owl	Чухъл	
214.	*Bubo bubo*	Eagle Owl	Бухал	
215.	*Glaucidium passerinum*	Pygmy Owl	Малка кукумявка	
216.	*Athene noctua*	Little Owl	Домашна кукумявка	
217.	*Strix aluco*	Tawny Owl	Горска улулица	
218.	*Strix uralensis*	Ural Owl	Уралска улулица	
219.	*Asio otus*	Long-eared Owl	Ушата сова	
220.	*Asio flammeus*	Short-eared Owl	Блатна сова	
221.	*Aegolius funereus*	Tengmalm's Owl	Пернатонога кукумявка	
222.	*Caprimulgus europaeus*	Nightjar	Козодой	
223.	*Apus apus*	Swift	Черен бързолет	
224.	*Apus pallidus*	Pallid Swift	Блед бързолет	
225.	*Apus melba*	Alpine Swift	Алпийски бързолет	
226.	*Alcedo atthis*	Kingfisher	Земеродно рибарче	
227.	*Merops superciliosus*	Blue-cheeked Bee-eater	Зелен пчелояд	
228.	*Merops apiaster*	Bee-eater	Обикновен пчелояд	
229.	*Coracias garrulus*	Roller	Синявица	
230.	*Upupa epops*	Hoopoe	Папуняк	
231.	*Jynx torquilla*	Wryneck	Въртошийка	

232.	*Picus canus*	Grey-headed Woodpecker	Сив кълвач	
233.	*Picus viridis*	Green Woodpecker	Зелен кълвач	
234.	*Dryocopus martius*	Black Woodpecker	Черен кълвач	
235.	*Dendrocopos major*	Great Spotted Woodpecker	Голям пъстър кълвач	
236.	*Dendrocopos syriacus*	Syrian Woodpecker	Сирийски кълвач	
237.	*Dendrocopos medius*	Middle Spotter Woodpecker	Среден пъстър кълвач	
238.	*Dendrocopos leucotus*	White-backed Woodpecker	Белогръб кълвач	
239.	*Dendrocopos minor*	Lesser Spotted Woodpecker	Малък пъстър кълвач	
240.	*Picoides tridactylus*	Three-toed Woodpecker	Трипръст кълвач	
241.	*Melanocorypha calandra*	Calandra Lark	Дебелоклюна чучулига	
242.	*Melanocorypha leucoptera*	White-winged Lark	Белокрила чучулига	
243.	*Melanocorypha yeltoniensis*	Black Lark	Черна чучулига	
244.	*Calandrella brachydactyla*	Short-toed Lark	Късопръста чучулига	
245.	*Calandrella rufescens*	Lesser Short-toed Lark	Сива чучулига	
246.	*Galerida cristata*	Crested Lark	Качулата чучулига	
247.	*Lullula arborea*	Woodlark	Горска чучулига	
248.	*Alauda arvensis*	Skylark	Полска чучулига	
249.	*Eremophila alpestris*	Shore Lark	Ушата чучулига	
250.	*Riparia riparia*	Sand Martin	Брегова лястовица	
251.	*Ptyonoprogne rupestris*	Crag Martin	Скална лястовица	
252.	*Hirundo rustica*	Swallow	Селска лястовица	
253.	*Hirundo daurica*	Red-rumped Swallow	Червенокръста лястовица	
254.	*Delichon urbica*	House Martin	Градска лястовица	
255.	*Anthus richardi*	Richard's Pipit	Степна бъбрица	
256.	*Anthus campestris*	Tawny Pipit	Полска бъбрица	
257.	*Anthus trivialis*	Tree Pipit	Горска бъбрица	

258.	*Anthus pratensis*	Meadow Pipit	Ливадна бъбрица	
259.	*Anthus cervinus*	Red-throated Pipit	Тундрова бъбрица	
260.	*Anthus spinoletta*	Water Pipit	Водна бъбрица	
261.	*Motacilla flava*	Yellow Wagtail	Жълта стърчиопашка	
262.	*Motacilla citreola*	Citrine Wagtail	Жълтоглава стърчиопашка	
263.	*Motacilla cinerea*	Grey Wagtail	Планинска стърчиопашка	
264.	*Motacilla alba*	Pied Wagtail	Бяла стърчиопашка	
265.	*Bombycilla garrulus*	Waxwing	Копринарка	
266.	*Cinclus cinclus*	Dipper	Воден кос	
267.	*Troglodytes troglodytes*	Wren	Орехче	
268.	*Prunella modularis*	Dunnock	Сивогуша завирушка	
269.	*Prunella collaris*	Alpine Accentor	Пъстрогуша завирушка	
270.	*Cercotrichas galactotes*	Rufous Bush Robin	Трънковче	
271.	*Erithacus rubecula*	Robin	Червеногушка	
272.	*Luscinia luscinia*	Thrush Nightingale	Северен славей	
273.	*Luscinia megarhynchos*	Nightingale	Южен славей	
274.	*Luscinia svecica*	Bluethroat	Синьогушка	
275.	*Phoenicurus ochruros*	Black Redstart	Домашна червеноопашка	
276.	*Phoenicurus phoenicurus*	Redstart	Градинска червеноопашка	
277.	*Saxicola rubetra*	Whinchat	Ръждивогушо ливадарче	
278.	*Saxicola torquata*	Stonechat	Черногушо ливадарче	
279.	*Saxicola maura*	Siberian Stonechat	Сибирско ливадарче	
280.	*Oenanthe isabellina*	Isabelline Wheatear	Ориенталско каменарче	
281.	*Oenanthe oenanthe*	Northern Wheatear	Сиво каменарче	
282.	*Oenanthe pleschanka*	Pied Wheatear	Черногърбо каменарче	
283.	*Oenanthe hispanica*	Black-eared Wheatear	Испанско каменарче	

284.	_Oenanthe finschii_	Finsch's Wheatear	Скално каменарче	
285.	_Oenanthe leucura_	Black Wheatear	Черно каменарче	
286.	_Monticola saxatilis_	Rock Thrush	Пъстър скален дрозд	
287.	_Monticola solitarius_	Blue Rock Thrush	Син скален дрозд	
288.	_Zoothera dauma_	White's Thrush	Златист дрозд	
289.	_Turdus torquatus_	Ring Ouzel	Белогуш дрозд	
290.	_Turdus merula_	Blackbird	Кос	
291.	_Turdus ruficollis_	Black-throated Thrush	Черногуш дрозд	
292.	_Turdus pilaris_	Fieldfare	Хвойнов дрозд	
293.	_Turdus philomelos_	Song Thrush	Поен дрозд	
294.	_Turdus iliacus_	Redwing	Белогуш дрозд	
295.	_Turdus viscivorus_	Mistle Thrush	Имелов дрозд	
296.	_Cettia cetti_	Cetti's Warbler	Свилено шаварче	
297.	_Cisticola juncidis_	Fan-tailed Warbler	Пъстроопашато шаварче	
298.	_Locustella naevia_	Grasshopper Warbler	Полски цвъркач	
299.	_Locustella fluviatilis_	River Warbler	Речен цвъркач	
300.	_Locustella luscinioides_	Savi's Warbler	Тръстиков цвъркач	
301.	_Acrocepnalus melanopogon_	Moustached Warbler	Мустакато шаварче	
302.	_Acrocephalus paludicola_	Aquatic Warbler	Водно шаварче	
303.	_Acrocephalus schoenobaenus_	Sedge Warbler	Крайбрежно шаварче	
304.	_Acrocephalus agricola_	Paddyfield Warbler	Индийско шаварче	
305.	_Acrocephalus dumetorum_	Blyth's Reed Warbler	Градинско шаварче	
306.	_Acrocephalus palustris_	Marsh Warbler	Храстово шаварче	
307.	_Acrocephalus scirpaceus_	Reed Warbler	Блатно шаварче	
308.	_Acrocephalus arundinaceus_	Great Reed Warbler	Тръстиково шаварче	
309.	_Hippolais pallida_	Olivaceous Warbler	Малък маслинов присмехулник	

310.	*Hippolais olivetorum*	Olive-tree Warbler	Голям маслинов присмехулник	
311.	*Hippolais icterina*	Icterine Warbler	Градински присмехулник	
312.	*Sylvia undata*	Dartford Warbler	Пъстрогушо коприварче	
313.	*Sylvia cantillans*	Subalpine Warbler	Червеногушо коприварче	
314.	*Sylvia melanocephala*	Sardinian Warbler	Малко черноглаво коприварче	
315.	*Sylvia hortensis*	Orphean Warbler	Орфеево коприварче	
316.	*Sylvia nisoria*	Barred Warbler	Ястребогушо коприварче	
317.	*Sylvia curruca*	Lesser Whitethroat	Малко белогушо коприварче	
318.	*Sylvia communis*	Whitethroat	Голямо белогушо коприварче	
319.	*Sylvia borin*	Garden Warbler	Градинско коприварче	
320.	*Sylvia atricapilla*	Blackcap	Голямо черноглаво	
321.	*Phylloscopus borealis*	Arctic Warbler	Северен певец	
322.	*Phylloscopus bonelli*	Bonelli's Warbler	Планински певец	
323.	*Phylloscopus sibilatrix*	Wood Warbler	Буков певец	
324.	*Phylloscopus collybita*	Chiffchaff	Елов певец	
325.	*Phylloscopus trochilus*	Willow Warbler	Брезов певец	
326.	*Regulus regulus*	Goldcrest	Жълтоглаво кралче	
327.	*Regulus ignicapillus*	Firecrest	Червеноглаво кралче	
328.	*Muscicapa striata*	Spotted Flycatcher	Сива мухоловка	
329.	*Ficedula parva*	Red-breasted Flycatcher	Червеногуша мухоловка	
330.	*Ficedula semitorquata*	Semi-collared Flycatcher	Полубеловрата мухоловка	
331.	*Ficedula albicollis*	Collared Flycatcher	Беловрата мухоловка	
332.	*Ficedula hypoleuca*	Pied Flycatcher	Жалобна мухоловка	
333.	*Panurus biarmicus*	Bearded Tit	Мустакат синигер	
334.	*Aegithalos caudatus*	Long-tailed Tit	Дългоопашат синигер	
335.	*Parus palustris*	Marsh Tit	Лъскавоглав синигер	

336.	*Parus lugubris*	Sombre Tit	Жалобен синигер	
337.	*Parus montanus*	Willow Tit	Матовоглав синигер	
338.	*Parus cristatus*	Crested Tit	Качулат синигер	
339.	*Parus ater*	Coal Tit	Черен синигер	
340.	*Parus caeruleus*	Blue Tit	Син синигер	
341.	*Parus major*	Great Tit	Голям синигер	
342.	*Sitta europaea*	Nuthatch	Горска зидарка	
343.	*Sitta neumayer*	Rock Nuthatch	Скална зидарка	
344.	*Tichodroma muraria*	Wallcreeper	Скалолазка	
345.	*Certhia familiaris*	Treecreeper	Горска дърволазка	
346.	*Certhia brachydactyla*	Short-toed Treecreeper	Градинска дърволазка	
347.	*Remiz pendulinus*	Penduline Tit	Торбогнезден синигер	
348.	*Oriolus oriolus*	Golden Oriole	Авлига	
349.	*Lanius collurio*	Red-backed Shrike	Червеногърба сврачка	
350.	*Lanius minor*	Lesser Grey Shrike	Черночела сврачка	
351.	*Lanius excubitor*	Great Grey Shrike	Сива сврачка	
352.	*Lanius senator*	Woodchat Shrike	Червеноглава сврачка	
353.	*Lanius nubicus*	Masked Shrike	Белочела сврачка	
354.	*Garrulus glandarius*	Jay	Сойка	
355.	*Pica pica*	Magpie	Сврака	
356.	*Nucifraga caryocatactes*	Nutcracker	Сокерица	
357.	*Pyrrhocorax graculus*	Alpine Chough	Жълтоклюна гарга	
358.	*Corvus monedula*	Jackdaw	Чавка	
359.	*Corvus frugilegus*	Rook	Полска врана	
360.	*Corvus corone cornix*	Hooded Crow	Сива врана	
361.	*Corvus corax*	Raven	Гарван	

362.	_Sturnus vulgaris_	Starling	Обикновен скорец	
363.	_Sturnus roseus_	Rose-coloured Starling	Розов скорец	
364.	_Passer domesticus_	House Sparrow	Домашно врабче	
365.	_Passer hispaniolensis_	Spanish Sparrow	Испанско врабче	
366.	_Passer italiae_	Italian Sparrow	Италианско врабче	
367.	_Passer montanus_	Tree Sparrow	Полско врабче	
368.	_Petronia petronia_	Rock Sparrow	Скално врабче	
369.	_Montifringilla nivalis_	Snow Finch	Снежна чинка	
370.	_Fringilla coelebs_	Chaffinch	Обикновена чинка	
371.	_Fringilla montifringilla_	Brambling	Планинска чинка	
372.	_Serinus serinus_	Serin	Диво канарче	
373.	_Carduelis chloris_	Greenfinch	Зеленика	
374.	_Carduelis carduelis_	Goldfinch	Щиглец	
375.	_Carduelis spinus_	Siskin	Елшова скатия	
376.	_Carduelis cannabina_	Linnet	Обикновено конопарче	
377.	_Carduelis flavirostris_	Twite	Жълтоклюно конопарче	
378.	_Carduelis flammea_	Redpoll	Брезова скатия	
379.	_Loxia leucoptera_	Two-barred Crossbill	Белокрила кръсточовка	
380.	_Loxia curvirostra_	Crossbill	Обикновена кръсточовка	
381.	_Rhodospiza obsoleta_	Desert Finch	Пустинна чинка	
382.	_Carpodacus erythrinus_	Scarlet Rosefinch	Червена чинка	
383.	_Pyrrhula pyrrhula_	Bullfinch	Червенушка	
384.	_Coccothraustes coccothraustes_	Hawfinch	Черешарка	
385.	_Calcarius lapponicus_	Lapland Bunting	Лапландска овесарка	
386.	_Plectrophenax nivalis_	Snow Bunting	Снежна овесарка	
387.	_Emberiza leucocephalos_	Pine Bunting	Белоглава овесарка	

388.	*Emberiza citrinella*	Yellowhammer	Жълта овесарка	
389.	*Emberiza cirlus*	Cirl Bunting	Черногърла овесарка	
390.	*Emberiza cia*	Rock Bunting	Сивоглава овесарка	
391.	*Emberiza hortulana*	Ortolan Bunting	Градинска овесарка	
392.	*Emberiza caesia*	Cretzschmar's Bunting	Пепелява овесарка	
393.	*Emberiza rustica*	Rustic Bunting	Белогуша овесарка	
394.	*Emberiza pusilla*	Little Bunting	Малка овесарка	
395.	*Emberiza schoeniclus*	Reed Bunting	Тръстикова овесарка	
396.	*Emberiza melanocephala*	Black-headed Bunting	Черноглава овесарка	
397.	*Miliaria calandra*	Corn Bunting	Сива овесарка	

Notes:

1. Species whit scientific name put in brackets are most probably escaped birds.
2. Species marked with * are extinct from Bulgaria, and no confirmed records have been made during the last century.
3. Underlined are the breeding species.

178

CURRENT TITLES FROM PENSOFT

(All titles are published in English)

Bulgarian Antarctic Research. Life Sciences *by V. Golemansky & N.Chipev (eds.).* ISBN 954-642-014-X. *December, 1996*, format 165X235, paperback, iv + 127 pp., 21 figs, 7 maps, 22 tables, 71 photos.

Bibliographia Trichopterorum. A World Bibliography of Trichoptera (Insecta) with Indexes. Volume 1. 1961-1970 *by Andrew P. Nimmo.* ISBN 954-642-012-3 *(PENSOFT Series Faunistica No. 5).* *November 1996*, format 165x235, paperback, viii + 597 pp.

The Game and the Man. *Proceedings of the XXII Congress of the International Union of Game Biologists, Sofia, 1995 by N. Botev (ed.).* ISBN 954-642-013-1. *October 1996*, format 165x235, paperback, xvi + 531 pp., 217 figs, 29 maps, 107 tables, 46 photos.

Where to Watch Birds in Bulgaria *by P. Yankov.* ISBN 954-642-011-5. *December 1996*, format 135x215, paperback, 40 line drawings of birds, 40 maps, vii + 179 pp.

Catalogue of the Linyphiid Spiders of Northern Asia (Arachnida, Araneae, Linyphiidae) *by K. Y. Eskov.* ISBN 954-642-001-8. *(PENSOFT Series Faunistica No 1).* 1994, format 145x205, paperback, 144 pp., 1 map.

Catalogue of the Ground-beetles of Bulgaria (Coleoptera: Carabidae) *by V. B. Gueorguiev and B. V. Gueorguiev.* ISBN 954-642-003-4 *(PENSOFT Series Faunistica No 2).* 1995, format 165x235, paperback, 279 pp., 1 map.

A Checklist of the Ground-beetles of Russia & Adjacent Lands (Insecta, Coleoptera, Carabidae) *by O. L. Kryzhanovskij, I. A. Belousov, I. I. Kabak, B. M. Kataev, K. V. Makarov, V. G. Shilenkov.* ISBN 954-642-003-4 *(PENSOFT Series Faunistica No 3).* 1995, format 205x290, paperback, 271 pp., 3 maps.

Reclassification of World Dyschiriini with a Revision of the Palearctic Fauna (Coleoptera, Carabidae) *by D. N. Fedorenko.* ISBN 954-642-009-3 *(PENSOFT Series Faunistica No 4).* 1996, format 205x290, paperback, 224 pp, 81 map, 328 figs.

Bulgarian Environmental Projects, 1992-1995 *by L. Cholpanova, N. Kazanski & R. Tsacheva.* ISBN 954-642-008-5.1996, format 145x205, paperback, 157 pp.

Ecosystem & Egosystem Evolution *by V. A. Krassilov.* ISBN 954-642-002-6. 1995, format 145x200, paperback, 172 pp.

Amphibian Populations of the Commonwealth of Independent States: Current status & Declines *by S. L. Kuzmin, S. C. Dodd & M. M. Pikulik (eds.)* ISBN 954-642-007-7. 1995, format 145x215, paperback, 157 pp., 11 maps, 25 tables, 8 figs.

Advances in Holocene Palaeoecology in Bulgaria *by E. Bozilova, S. Tonkov (eds.)* ISBN 954-642-005-0. 1995, format 145x210, paperback, vii+109 pp. 28 figs, 2 maps, 1 table, English text.

Co-evolution of the tamarisks (Tamaricaceae) & pest arthropods (Insecta; Arachnida; Acarina), with special reference to biological control prospects *by O. V. Kovalev.* ISBN 954-642-006-9. *Proceedings of the Zoological Institute of the Russian Academy of Sciences at St. Petersburg, vol. 259.* 1995, paperback, 110 pp, 1 table, 2 maps, 20 figs.

FORTHCOMING TITLES

Guide to the Butterflies of Russia and Adjacent Territories (Lepidoptera, Rhopalocera). Volume 1: Hesperiidae, Papilionidae, Pieridae, Satyridae *by P. V. Bogdanov, A. L. Devyatkin, L. V. Kabak, V. A. Korolev, V. S. Murzin, G. D. Samodurov, E. A. Tarasov, and V. K. Tuzov.* ISBN 954-642-018-2. Format 220x290, appr. 400 pp., richly illustrated by color photos and plates, hardcover.

Advances in Amphibian Research in the Former Soviet Union *by S. L. Kuzmin & S. C. Dodd, Jr. (eds.).* ISSN 1310-8840. Volume 1. ISBN 954-642-017-4. Format 165X235, paperback, appr. 250 pp., many tables, figs, color photos, maps.

Angiosperm Origins: Morphological and Ecological Aspects *by V. A. Krassilov.* ISBN 954-642-016-6. Format 145x200, paperback, appr. 240 pp., many tables, figs, maps, ca. 600 original photographs of various plant fossils, with a very rich bibliography as well (about 500 citations).

Natural Zeolites. *Proceedings of the International Meeting on Zeolites, Sofia by G. Kirov, O. Petrov & L. Filizova (eds.).* ISBN 954-642-015-8. Format 165X235, paperback, appr. 330 pp., many tables, figs.

In 1997 appears:

Guide to the butterflies of Russia and adjacent territories (Lepidoptera, Rhopalocera). Volume 1: Hesperiidae, Papilionidae, Pieridae, Satyridae

by

P. V. Bogdanov, A. L. Devyatkin, L. V. Kabak, V. A. Korolev, V. S. Murzin, G. D. Samodurov, E. A. Tarasov, and V. K. Tuzov

A unique, long-needed, full-colour edition devoted to a relatively popular, guide-like assessment of four most beautiful butterfly families in the scope of the fauna of the entire former Soviet Union (FSU). A historical review is provided of lepidopterological research and of some of its key figures in Russia, dating back to the early 18th century. Altogether, over 400 butterfly species or subspecies, including four Central Asian species new to science, are documented from the FSU, each supplied with a brief account of its taxonomy, status, ecology, biology, variability, and distribution. Virtually each taxon is illustrated by 1:1 colour photographs of the male and female both from upperside and beneath, with several old and new type specimens involved. In the cases of sibling/similar forms, their genitalic distinguishing characters are depicted as well. Based on butterfly distribution patterns, a general zoogeographical division of the FSU is proposed. In addition, several dozen beautiful photographs display a number of habitats/landscapes supporting some most interesting/picturesque butterflies in the FSU. Destined for professional and amateur entomologists, all lovers of butterflies and Nature. Altogether perhaps ca. 400 pages of A4 format, hardcover.

For order details please contact:

Dr. Lyubomir Penev
PENSOFT Publishers
Akad. G. Bonchev Str. Bl. 6
1113 Sofia, Bulgaria
Tel/Fax +359-2-7133460
E-mail: pensoft@main.infotel.bg